Dietrich | Untertrifaller

Editorial

Die Buchreihe *De aedibus international* gibt uns die Möglichkeit, Streiflichter auf die Werke einzelner Architekten zu werfen und dabei bemerkenswerte Bauten, eine spezifische architektonische Haltung und die zugehörigen Biografien der Architekten kennenzulernen.
Bei Helmut Dietrich und Much Untertrifaller begegnen wir einem bereits umfangreichen Werk, an dessen Anfang ein Grossauftrag, die Erweiterung des Bregenzer Festspielhauses, steht. Mit dem frühen, vielbeachteten Wettbewerbserfolg – die Architekten waren damals 33 und 35 Jahre alt – wurden sie Teil der bereits international bekannten, scharf umrissenen Architekturszene Vorarlbergs. In der Folge konnten sie ihr Werk sukzessive weiterentwickeln und ausbauen. Erscheint beispielsweise das Festspielhaus in Bregenz äusserlich noch karg und sachlich, wandelt sich im Innern der Ausdruck; die Räume strahlen eine ausserordentliche Grandezza und Poesie aus. Die Stadthalle F in Wien erfährt nun auch im Äusseren eine souveräne und festliche Geste, die dem öffentlichen Gebäude angemessen ist und auch hier wieder festlichen Innenräumen entspricht. Einige der in diesem Band versammelten Bauten befinden sich in suburbanen Bereichen, wo Landschaft und Stadt aufeinandertreffen. Das hat das Sensorium der zwei Architekten für den spezifischen Ort geschärft. So wird etwa das ETH Sport Center am Rand des dicht bebauten Hochschul-Campus auf dem Hönggerberg in Zürich zu einer begrünten Terrasse, unter der die grosse Sporthalle und die nötigen Nebenräume gleichsam verschwinden. Diese Disposition folgt dem Wunsch nach grösstmöglichem Respekt gegenüber der weiträumigen Landschaft rund um den Campus. Mit ähnlicher Sorgfalt gegenüber der Topografie verfahren die Architekten beim Reka-Feriendorf in Urnäsch im Kanton Appenzell. Mit der Abtreppung der drei Wohnflügel passt sich die Anlage präzise der leichten Neigung des Terrains an. Der verbindende Trakt mit den Gemeinschaftsräumen akzentuiert gekonnt diese Stufung entlang des Hangs.
Die einzelnen Bände der Reihe bieten immer auch Gelegenheit für analytische Texte von Autoren, die sich mit dem Werk der Architekten vertieft auseinandersetzen. Hier ist es der langjährige Feuilletonredaktor der NZZ, Roman Hollenstein, der mit grossem Hintergrundwissen den Werdegang, die Bauten und das kulturelle Umfeld der Bregenzer Architekten spannend und eloquent beschreibt und beleuchtet.

Luzern, im Juni 2013 Heinz Wirz

Editorial

The *De aedibus international* series gives us the chance to shed light on the works of individual architects and thereby discover remarkable buildings and specific architectural stances, as well as learning about the architects' biographies.
In the case of Helmut Dietrich and Much Untertrifaller, we encounter an extensive amount of work, which began with a major contract, namely the extension to the Bregenz Festival House. With this early, high-profile competition success – at the time, the architects were 33 and 35 years old – they became part of the already internationally known, clearly outlined Vorarlberg architectural scene. After that, they were able to successively expand their work and develop it further. For instance while the outside of the Bregenz Festival House still appears to be sparse and clinical, its expression transforms inside: The rooms radiate an abundance of *grandezza* and poetry. By the time of the Stadthalle Wien project, it was also given a confident, festive gesture that is appropriate for a public building, while also presenting festive interior rooms. Some of the buildings compiled in this volume are located in suburban areas, where the landscape and the city meet. That has heightened the two architects' sensitivity for specific locations. For instance the ETH sports centre at the edge of the densely developed university campus on Hönggerberg in Zurich becomes a green terrace, beneath which the large sports hall and the required auxiliary rooms all disappear. That disposition follows the desire for the maximum possible respect towards the wide open landscape around the campus. The architects treat the topography of the Reka holiday village in Urnäsch, Appenzell with similar care. The three offset residential wings allow the facility to be precisely inserted into the incline of the terrain. The connecting wing with its common rooms skilfully accentuates that staggering along the slope.
The individual volumes of this series also always provide an opportunity for analytical texts by authors who have studied the architects' work in depth. In this case, it is the long-standing Arts Editor of the NZZ, Roman Hollenstein, who reveals his great background knowledge in excitingly and eloquently describing and illuminating the careers, the buildings and the cultural environment of these Bregenz architects.

Lucerne, June 2013 Heinz Wirz

8 De aedibus international

Dietrich | Untertrifaller
Bregenz

Quart Verlag Luzern

Dietrich | Untertrifaller
8. Band der Reihe De aedibus international/Volume 8 of the series De aedibus international

Herausgeber/Edited by: Heinz Wirz, Luzern
Konzept/Concept: Dietrich|Untertrifaller, Bregenz; Heinz Wirz
Textbeitrag/Article by: Roman Hollenstein, Zürich
Objekttexte/Project descriptions: Roman Hollenstein
Vorwort/Foreword: Heinz Wirz
Redaktion/Editing: Dietrich|Untertrifaller, Judith Wellmann
Übersetzung/English translation: Benjamin Liebelt, Berlin
Textlektorat Deutsch/Text editing German: Annika Greuter, Heidelberg
Fotos/Photos: Bruno Klomfar, Wien. Ausser/Except: Adolf Bereuter, Dornbirn, S./p. 8, 61, 63; Gert v. Bassewitz, Hamburg, S./p. 7; Ignacio Martinez, Navia, S./p. 8, 9, 12, 15, 58, 59; Christoph Kraneburg, Köln, S./p. 17; Darko Todorovic, Dornbirn, S./p. 62
Visualisierungen/Graphics: Expressiv, Wien, S./p. 16–17

Grafische Umsetzung/Graphic design: Quart Verlag, Linus Wirz
Lithos: Printeria, Luzern
Druck und Bindung/Printing and binding: DZA Druckerei zu Altenburg GmbH

ISBN 978-3-03761-063-3

Quart Verlag GmbH
Denkmalstrasse 2, CH-6006 Luzern
books@quart.ch, www.quart.ch

Weitsicht und Augenmass

Roman Hollenstein*

In Österreich waren Helmut Dietrich und Much Untertrifaller keine Unbekannten mehr, als sie mit dem nach einer zweistufigen Umbauphase im Sommer 2006 festlich eingeweihten Bregenzer Festspielhaus für weltweites Aufsehen sorgten. Bis heute gilt der mit präzisen baukünstlerischen Interventionen in ein einprägsames Gesamtkunstwerk verwandelte Musentempel, den Marc Forster 2008 in *Quantum of Solace* zur spektakulären Bühne für einen sportlich im Smoking agierenden James Bond machte, als das eigentliche Vorzeigewerk des international tätigen Bregenzer Architekturbüros. Das Ausgangsmaterial für diesen bald skulptural, bald technisch anmutenden Bau bildete das 1980 eröffnete Theaterhaus von Wilhelm Braun. Dieses bereits etwas angestaubt wirkende Gebäude holten Dietrich|Untertrifaller mit einem in 15 Metern Höhe zwischen dem bestehenden Bühnenturm und dem neuen Kubus der Werkstattbühne vermittelnden «Wolkenbügel» und dem teleskopartig über dem Haupteingang auskragenden Festsaal in die Gegenwart. Die einem additiven Prinzip verpflichtete Überformung von Brauns Bau kann man entfernt mit Palladios Basilica in Vicenza vergleichen, führte doch in beiden Fällen die Transformation bestehender Gebäude zu einem Werk von grosser Ausstrahlung. Much Untertrifaller betont denn auch: «Grenzen und Einschränkungen reizen uns. Denn wenn man alles darf, wird es unerträglich schwer.»[1]

Bauen in Vorarlberg

Bei ihrem komplexen Eingriff in die Substanz des alten Festspielhauses, aber auch bei anderen Umbauten war und ist Helmut Dietrich und Much Untertrifaller «ein einfühlsamer Umgang mit dem Bestand wichtig. Bei Brauns Altbau handelte es sich um eine qualitativ bescheidene, aber vom Bestand her riesige Architektur. Wir entschieden uns, diesem Grossvolumen kleine Einzelteile anzufügen und daraus eine neue Silhouette zu entwickeln.» (U) So ergab sich das skulptural unregelmässige Erscheinungsbild des Festspielhauses, das

Farsightedness and a Sense of Proportion

Roman Hollenstein*

Helmut Dietrich and Much Untertrifaller were already well known in Austria when they attracted worldwide attention with the two-stage conversion of the Bregenz Festival House, which was officially inaugurated in the summer of 2006. To this day, the dramatic venue that was transformed into an impressive *Gesamtkunstwerk* through precise architectural intervention, and which was used by Marc Forster in 2008 as a spectacular backdrop for a sporty, tuxedo-wearing James Bond in *Quantum of Solace*, is regarded as the showcase piece of the internationally operative Bregenz architectural office. The original material for the sometimes sculptural, sometimes technical appearance of the building was the theatre by Wilhelm Braun, which was opened in 1980. Dietrich|Untertrifaller gave the somewhat ragged looking building a contemporary appearance by using a "cloud hanger" at a height of 15 metres to mediate between the existing stage tower and the new cuboid of the workshop stage, as well as the telescopically projecting ballroom. The superstructure to Braun's building, which is based on an additive principle, is distantly comparable to Palladio's Basilica in Vicenza, since in both cases, the transformation of the existing building led to a work of great radiance. Much Untertrifaller also stresses: "We are inspired by boundaries and limitations. Because if anything goes, things become unbearably difficult."[1]

Building in Vorarlberg

While implementing the complex measures to the substance of the old Festival House, as well as in other conversions, Helmut Dietrich and Much Untertrifaller have always considered, "an empathetic treatment of the existing substance to be important. In the case of Braun's original building, its quality was modest, but the existing architecture was enormous. We decided to add small individual elements to this large volume and thereby develop a new silhouette." (U)

* *Roman Hollenstein* (1953) ist promovierter Kunst- und Architekturhistoriker. Er war zunächst für die Sammlungen des Fürsten von Liechtenstein in Vaduz und Wien tätig. Anschliessend arbeitete er als freier Ausstellungsmitarbeiter am Kunstmuseum Basel, erfüllte Lehraufträge an der Universität Bern und unterrichtete an der Hochschule für Gestaltung in Zürich. Von 1987 bis 1990 war er Direktionsmitglied des Schweizerischen Instituts für Kunstwissenschaft in Zürich. Seit 1990 ist er bei der Neuen Zürcher Zeitung in Zürich als Feuilleton-Redakteur für die Gebiete Architektur, Denkmalpflege und Design verantwortlich. Neben Aufsätzen und Kritiken in der Neuen Zürcher Zeitung publizierte er zur Kunst um 1800, zur zeitgenössischen Kunst und Architektur, zur Museumsarchitektur, zum Synagogenbau sowie zur Architektur in Israel. Seit 2003 ist er assoziiertes Mitglied des Bundes Schweizer Architekten (BSA). 2012 wurde er mit dem Preis für Architekturkritik des Bundes Deutscher Architekten (BDA) ausgezeichnet.

* *Roman Hollenstein* (1953) has a PhD in History of Art and Architecture. He initially took a position as a Research Assistant for the Collections of the Prince of Liechtenstein in Vaduz and Vienna. He then worked as a freelance exhibition staff member at the Kunstmuseum Basel, lectured at the University of Bern and taught at the Zurich University of the Arts. Between 1987 and 1990, he was a Board Member of the Art History Department of the Swiss Institute for Art Research in Zurich. Since 1990, he has worked for the Neue Zürcher Zeitung in Zurich, where he set up the Art Trade section and expanded the Architecture section. As an Arts Editor, he is responsible for the fields of architecture, monument preservation and design. In addition to essays and critiques in the Neue Zürcher Zeitung, he has published pieces on art around 1800, international contemporary art, Swiss art, contemporary Swiss architecture, museum architecture, synagogue building, and architecture in Israel. Since 2003, Roman Hollenstein has been an Associate Member of the Federation of Swiss Architects (BSA). In 2012, he was awarded the BDA Prize for Architecture Criticism.

Umbau/Conversion Altmann-Fabrik, Bregenz, 1996

verglichen mit anderen Werken von Dietrich|Untertrifaller fast schon barock anmutet, ganz aus der Funktion: «Wir stellten die Werkstattbühne als schwarze Box dazu und legten den Erschliessungsgang samt Büros oben als Riegel über das Gebäude. Ihm antwortet eine zweite, durchgesteckte Spange für Besucher, die auf niedrigerer Ebene das ganze Haus durchstösst und auf der Seeseite in einem Foyer endet. Diese beiden für die Mitarbeiter einerseits und die Besucher andererseits bestimmten Röhren, die sich an einer vom Speiselift definierten Achse treffen, erlaubten es uns, die ganze Logistik des riesigen Komplexes zu bewerkstelligen, ohne dass wir unterirdische Eingriffe tätigen mussten.» (D)
Bereits mit der ersten, 1997 abgeschlossenen Umbauetappe des Festspielhauses signalisierten Dietrich|Untertrifaller der Architekturszene, dass die Vorarlberger Baukunst mehr zu bieten hatte als jene kargen Einfamilienhäuser aus Holz, mit denen das westlichste Bundesland Österreichs seit den 1960er Jahren immer wieder auf sich aufmerksam machte. «Diese Entwicklung wurde von jungen Architekten und Handwerkern – darunter Hans Purin und Rudolf Wäger – getragen. Sie bauten kleine Häuser, die zunächst auf wenig Verständnis stiessen.» (D) Die systemkritische Gruppe der Vorarlberger Baukünstler bereitete mit ihrem kollektiv-partizipatorischen Planen und materialbewussten Bauen in den 1980er Jahren den Grund für das bis heute florierende Bauwesen zwischen Bodensee und Arlberg. Mit geringen Mitteln – und ohne viel Theorie – realisierten die Baukünstler einfache, aber überzeugende Gebäude und schufen so einen ethischen, aber auch ästhetischen Mehrwert. «Der Durchbruch war geschafft, als Hans Purin und die Baukünstler 1991 den Kulturpreis des Landes Vorarlberg erhielten.» (D) Seither gehört es im «Ländle» zum guten Ton, sich nicht nur Villen, Rathäuser und Schulen von namhaften Architekten errichten zu lassen, sondern auch Neubauten für Verwaltung, Industrie und Handwerk.

Erste Erfolge

Vorarlberg, das in den 1980er Jahren einen grossen baulichen Nachholbedarf hatte, bot damals jungen Architekten gute Entfaltungschancen – auch Helmut Dietrich und Much Untertrifaller, die beide an der Technischen Universität Wien studiert hatten und mitten in dieser Aufbruchszeit zu arbeiten begannen. «In jenen Jahren wurde die Vorarlberger Bauschule zum Selbstläufer. Ihre Werke wurden im Weichbild des Landes deutlich wahrnehmbar. Heute ist die neue Bauweise politisch und gesellschaftlich akzeptiert, zumal die Architekten auf eine enge Zusammenarbeit mit den Handwerkern setzen.» (D)

The result was a sculptural, irregular appearance for the Festival House, with an almost Baroque atmosphere compared to other works by Dietrich|Untertrifaller that is entirely derived from its function: "We added the workshop stage as a black box and placed the access walkway with offices at the top, as a bar above the building. A second, extended brace for visitors acts as a counterpart, penetrating the entire building at a low level and ending on the lake side in a foyer. These two tubes, one for staff and one for visitors, which meet at an axis defined by the catering lift, allowed us to implement the entire logistics of the enormous complex without having to use any underground measures." (D)
Even with the first stage of conversion to the Festival House, which was completed in 1997, Dietrich|Untertrifaller communicated to the architectural scene that Vorarlberg architecture has more to offer than the austere wooden single-family homes, with which the western-most state in Austria has regularly attracted attention since the 1960s. "That development was led by young architects and craftsmen – including Hans Purin and Rudolf Wäger. They built small houses that initially met with little enthusiasm." (D) The critical group of Vorarlberg architects in the 1980s, with their collective-participatory planning and materially aware building, paved the way for today's flourishing building culture between Lake Constance and Arlberg. They used limited means – and little theory – to build simple, yet convincing buildings, thereby creating added value both in terms of ethics and aesthetics. "The breakthrough was achieved in 1991, when Hans Purin and the architects were awarded the Cultural Prize of the State of Vorarlberg." (D) Since then, it has been a matter of esteem in the region to have renowned architects to design not only villas, town halls and schools, but also new buildings for administration, industry and craftsmanship.

Initial successes

Vorarlberg, which suffered from a great construction backlog in the 1980s, offered young architects a good opportunity to develop. Among them were Helmut Dietrich and Much Untertrifaller, who had both studied at the Vienna University of Technology and started their careers in the middle of that period of renewal. "In those years, the Vorarlberg school of architecture was an automatic success. Its works were clearly visible in the state's municipal landscape. Today, the construction method is politically and socially accepted, especially since the architects valued close collaboration with craftsmen." (D)
In 1986, Helmut Dietrich and Much Untertrifaller began working together on projects, "even though we

[1] Bei diesem und den folgenden Zitaten handelt es sich – wenn nicht anders angemerkt – um Auszüge aus einem Gespräch mit Helmut Dietrich und Much Untertrifaller vom 18. September 2012 in Bregenz. Die Aussagen von Helmut Dietrich sind am Schluss des Zitats mit (D), diejenigen von Much Untertrifaller mit (U) gekennzeichnet.

[1] Unless otherwise stated, this and all following quotes are extracts from a discussion with Helmut Dietrich and Much Untertrifaller in Bregenz on September 18, 2012. Statements by Helmut Dietrich are marked (D) at the end of the quote, while those by Much Untertrifaller are marked (U).

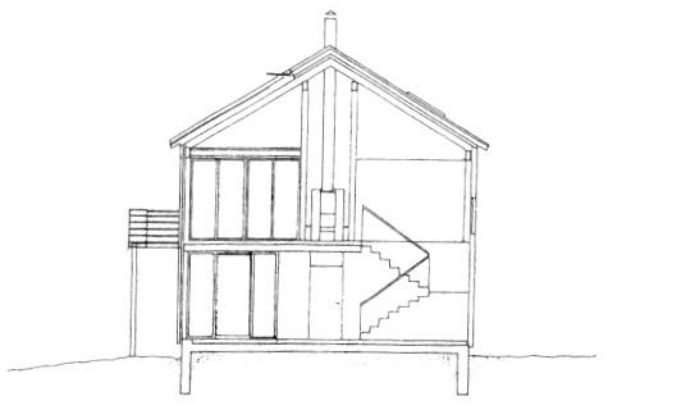

Haus/House P, Schnepfau, 1989

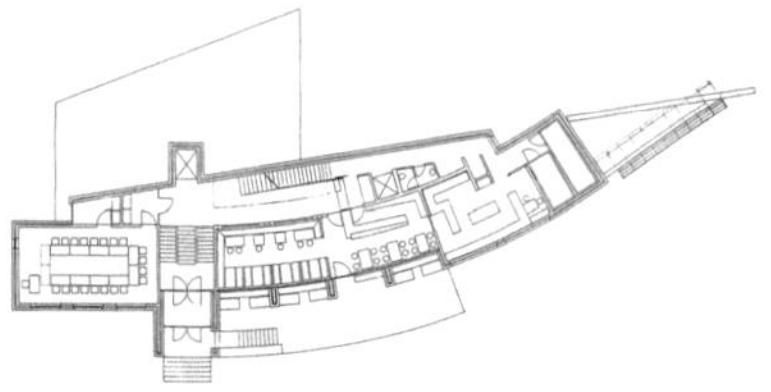

Silvrettahaus Bielerhöhe/House Silvretta Bielerhöhe, Gaschurn, 1992

Bürogebäude/Office building, Rupp Cheese Innovation, Lochau, 1998

Walch's Event Catering, Lustenau, 2000

Im Jahr 1986 begannen Helmut Dietrich und Much Untertrifaller gemeinsam zu projektieren, «auch wenn wir daneben noch in anderen Bürogemeinschaften tätig waren: Helmut arbeitete mit Hermann Kaufmann und Christian Lenz zusammen und ich mit meinem Vater.» (U) Einen ersten Erfolg verzeichnete Helmut Dietrich 1989 mit dem die ländliche Baukunst seiner Bregenzerwälder Heimat neu interpretierenden Haus Preuss in Schnepfau, dessen Eingangsveranda er vom traditionellen «Schopf» hergeleitet hatte. Drei Jahre später realisierte Much Untertrifaller gemeinsam mit seinem Vater (Much Untertrifaller sen.) und Gerhard Hörburger das viel beachtete, in freiem Schwung über dem Bielerhöhe-Stausee sich zur Gebirgslandschaft hin öffnende Silvrettahaus in Gaschurn. «Schnell haben Much und ich Wettbewerbe gewonnen, aus denen aber nicht immer etwas geworden ist. Die Konkurrenz war klein, denn in den späten 1980er Jahren nahmen auch bei grossen Ausschreibungen selten mehr als fünf bis zehn Büros teil, da die meisten jungen Kollegen sich aufs ‹Hüslebauen› beschränkten.» (D) Dennoch galt 1992 ihr Sieg im Festspielhaus-Wettbewerb als kleine Sensation. Im Hinblick auf die Realisierung des ersten Bauabschnitts gründeten sie 1994 ein gemeinsames Büro in Bregenz, dem bald Niederlassungen in Wien und St. Gallen folgten.

Parallel zum Bregenzer Grossauftrag, der sich bis 2006 hinzog, widmeten sie sich mit Experimentierlust der gesamten Palette der damals in Vorarlberg anstehenden Bauaufgaben: vom Ein- und Mehrfamilienhaus über Schul- und Sportbauten bis hin zu Verwaltungs- und Industriegebäuden. So findet man die elegante Rhetorik des Festspielhauses im 1998 eröffneten Firmensitz von Rupp Cheese Innovation in Lochau wieder, einem elegant über einem Steinsockel schwebenden Glaspavillon mit seitlicher Metallhülle. Das zwei Jahre später vollendete kistenartige Produktionsgebäude von Walch's Event Catering in Lustenau hingegen wurde dank der vom Innsbrucker Künstler Peter Kogler bildhaft gestalteten Hülle zur minimalistisch-kistenartigen Skulptur. Kann man dieses Werk, dessen architektonische Aussage sich hauptsächlich zum Innenhof hin orientiert, als baukünstlerische Fingerübung bezeichnen, so handelt es sich bei den zwischen 1998 und 2000 vollendeten Kindergärten in Lustenau, Wolfurt und Lauterach um zukunftsweisende Neuformulierungen der Holzarchitektur. Einen formalen Vorläufer zu diesen auf den besonnten Längsseiten verglasten Pavillonbauten mit zentralen oder nordseitigen Erschliessungskorridoren kann man im 1996 am Fuss der Bregenzer Oberstadt realisierten Haus Bautz erkennen.

Wie für viele erfolgreiche Architekten ist das Einfamilienhaus auch für Dietrich|Untertrifaller ein ideales

also worked for other partnerships: Helmut collaborated with Hermann Kaufmann and Christian Lenz, and I worked with my father." (U) Helmut Dietrich was initially successful in 1989 with his *Haus Preuss* in Schnepfau, which reinterpreted the rural architecture of his native Bregenzwald, deriving its entrance veranda from the traditional "crest". Three years later, Much Untertrifaller, his father (Much Untertrifaller Sr.) and Gerhard Hörburger produced the widely renowned *Silvrettahaus* in Gaschurn, which was designed with liberal panache above the Silvretta reservoir. "Much and I quickly won competitions, which however didn't always come to anything. There was limited competition, because in the late 1980s, hardly more than five or ten offices participated even in major tender invitations, since most young colleagues confined themselves to building single family homes." (D) Evenso, in 1992, winning the Festival House competition was regarded as a minor sensation. To implement the first construction phase, they founded a joint office in Bregenz in 1994, which was soon followed by branches in Vienna and St. Gallen.

In parallel with the major assignment in Bregenz, which lasted until 2006, they also dedicated themselves with an experimental zeal to the entire range of construction tasks that were required in Vorarlberg at the time: including single family homes and apartment buildings, school and sports facilities, and industrial plants. Thus it is possible to find the elegant rhetoric of the Festival House in the corporate headquarters of Rupp Cheese Innovation in Lochau, which was opened in 1998. It is an elegant glass pavilion floating above a stone base, with a lateral metal shell. Completed two years later, the production building for Walch's Event Catering in Lustenau was designed as a minimalist, case-like sculpture thanks to the visually conceived shell by the artist Peter Kogler. While one could describe this building, which has an architectural expression that is mainly oriented towards the interior courtyard, as an architectural five-finger exercise, the kindergartens in Lustenau, Wolfurt and Lauterach that were completed between 1998 and 2000 are forward-looking reformulations of wooden architecture. These glazed pavilion buildings with sunlit lateral sides are formal successors to the *Haus Bautz,* which was built in 1996 at the foot of the Bregenz upper town.

As for many architects, single family homes are an ideal field of experimentation for Dietrich|Untertrifaller: "They allow us to test things out before we apply them to larger buildings. We love working in different scales and therefore develop major construction projects with as much pleasure as we do homes and furniture." (D) They proved that already

Experimentierfeld: «Hier können wir Dinge ausprobieren, bevor wir sie bei grösseren Bauten anwenden. Wir lieben es, in verschiedenen Massstäben zu arbeiten, und entwickeln deshalb genauso gerne Grossbauten und Einfamilienhäuser wie Möbel.» (D) Das bewiesen sie schon 1996 bei der Neugestaltung der Cafébar «Greil» in Innsbruck, der ersten Arbeit, die sie ausserhalb Vorarlbergs realisieren konnten. Ebenfalls in Tirol entstand dann zwischen 1999 und 2001 das Wellnessbad und Veranstaltungszentrum St. Anton am Arlberg, eine teilweise in den Hang hineingeschobene Anlage, deren begrünte Dachflächen durch schachtelartige Oberlichter akzentuiert werden.
Beim 2003 eingeweihten Inatura-Museum in Dornbirn führte die Auseinandersetzung mit der Altbausubstanz, die seit dem Wettbewerb für das Bregenzer Festspielhaus eine wichtige Stellung im Schaffen von Dietrich|Untertrifaller einnimmt, erneut zu einer eigenwilligen Lösung. Zusammen mit Hermann Kaufmann und Christian Lenz verwandelten sie die ehemaligen Rüschwerke in ein naturgeschichtliches Museum mit angegliedertem Kunstraum, indem sie die Fabrikanlage um einen Verbindungsbau sowie zwei Büropavillons erweiterten. Diese verpackten sie in transparente, mit Rost-Mustern bedruckte Textilhüllen, welche – über dem verglasten Erdgeschoss schwebend – entfernt an ihre Lustenauer Bauskulptur erinnern.
Im gleichen Jahr konnten Dietrich|Untertrifaller mit dem Neubau der Hauptschule im vorarlbergischen Klaus die erste Passivhaus-Schule Österreichs vollenden – dank einer Tragkonstruktion aus vorgefertigten Holzteilen in nur anderthalb Jahren Bauzeit. Das augenfälligste Merkmal des Gebäudes ist der vorgesetzte «Schleier» aus gelochtem Kupfertrapezblech, der die südseitige Fensterfront des Foyers und der Bibliothek vor direktem Sonnenlicht schützt. Dasselbe Material verwendeten Dietrich|Untertrifaller wenig später bei der Eurospar-Filiale Vorkloster in Bregenz, wo es nicht nur die Glasfassade verschattet, sondern als hochgeschobenes «Fallgitter» auch als weithin sichtbare, zeichenhafte Scheinfassade dient.

Wettbewerbskultur

Solche Bauten, bei denen Dietrich|Untertrifaller auf «Fortschritt mit Augenmass setzen» (D), festigten ihren Ruf und führten bald schon dazu, dass sie mit Aufträgen überhäuft wurden. Dennoch nahm und nimmt ihr Büro weiterhin an Wettbewerben teil – seit dem Jahr 2000 auch in der Schweiz, wo es den Auftrag für ein Reka-Feriendorf in Urnäsch im Kanton Appenzell Ausserrhoden erhielt und sich vier Jahre später mit dem prestigeträchtigen Projekt einer neuen Hochschulsportanlage der ETH Zürich auf dem Hönggerberg gegen illustre Konkurrenten durchsetzen

in 1996 with the conversion of the café bar *Greil* in Innsbruck, the first work that they implemented outside Vorarlberg. Another project in Tirol, which was constructed between 1999 and 2001, was the spa and event centre in St. Anton am Arlberg, a facility that was partially inserted into the slope and had green rooftops that were accentuated with box-like skylights.
At the Inatura Museum, which was inaugurated in Dornbirn in 2003, study of the old building's substance – a priority for Dietrich|Untertrifaller ever since the Bregenz Festival House competition – once again led to an unconventional solution. Together with Hermann Kaufmann and Christian Lenz, they transformed the former *Rüsch-Werke* industrial estate into a natural history museum with an adjoining art gallery, by extending the factory estate to include a connecting building and two pavilion offices. They wrapped them in a rust-patterned, printed textile shell – hovering above the glazed ground floor – as distant echoes of their Lustenau architectural sculpture.
The same year, Dietrich|Untertrifaller completed Austria's first passive-house school building with a building for the secondary school in Klaus, Vorarlberg – needing a construction period of only one and a half years due to a load-bearing structure consisting of prefabricated wooden parts. The most eye-catching characteristic of the building is the draped "veil" of perforated copper sheet metal, which protects the southern window front of the foyer and the library from direct sunlight. Dietrich|Untertrifaller used the same material a little later for the Eurospar store in Bregenz-Vorkloster, where it not only acts as a shade for the glass façade, but also as a raised "portcullis" to present a false façade that is visible from afar.

Competition culture

Such buildings, in which Dietrich|Untertrifaller focus on "progress with proportion" (D), consolidated their reputation and quickly led to a flood of contracts. Nevertheless, their office has always continued to participate in competitions – also in Switzerland since 2000, where they immediately won the competition for a Reka holiday village in Urnäsch in the canton of Appenzell Ausserrhoden. Four years later, they were awarded the prestigious project for a new university sports facility at the ETH Zurich on the Hönggerberg, overcoming illustrious competitors. Their clever urban planning placed the sports facility, which was completed in 2009, at the eastern edge of the campus. The building faces the campus with a glass façade that has an urban character, while towards the hill – like the complex in St. Anton – the building becomes part of the landscape. "The geometry of the ETH

Kindergarten Wiesenweg, Wolfurt, 2000

Kindergarten Rosenlächerstrasse, Lustenau, 1999

Haus/House B, Bregenz, 1996

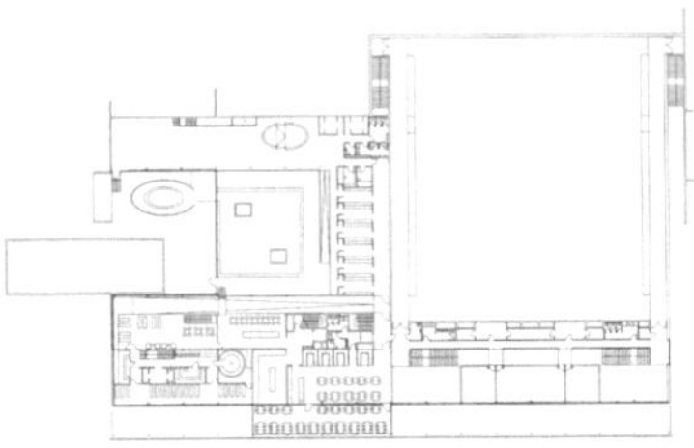

Veranstaltungshalle und Wellnessbad/
Event hall and spa, St. Anton, 2001

2 Helmut Dietrich und Much Untertrifaller 2005 in einem Interview mit Wojciech Czaja in Wien.

2 Helmut Dietrich and Much Untertrifaller in an interview with Wojciech Czaja in Vienna in 2005.

konnte. Die 2009 vollendete Sportanlage platzierten sie urbanistisch geschickt am Ostrand des Campus. Diesem wendet der Bau seine städtisch wirkende Glasfassade zu, während er zum Hügel hin – ähnlich wie der Baukomplex in St. Anton – Teil der Landschaft wird. «Die Geometrie des ETH-Projekts ist nämlich ganz aus der Hangtopografie hergeleitet, auf die wir mit einem System aus Rechtecken, Dreiecken und Parallelogrammen antworteten.» (D)
Doch nicht alle Schweizer Wettbewerbsprojekte waren erfolgreich. So mussten sie sich bei ihren 2003 eingereichten Vorschlägen für die Neugestaltung des Rorschacher Hafengeländes, für das neue Casino Basel und für die Transformation des Theaters 11 in Zürich mit undankbaren zweiten oder dritten Plätzen begnügen. Dabei hätte der weit ausladende neokubistische Baukörper des Theaters 11 zu einem attraktiven Aushängeschild für Zürichs Stadtquartier Oerlikon werden können, stellte doch dessen entfernt an Rem Koolhaas' Casa da Música in Porto erinnernder Entwurf eine eigenwillig zwischen Minimalismus und Barock oszillierende Weiterentwicklung der 2002 konzipierten und 2005 vollendeten Musik- und Veranstaltungshalle F in Wien dar.
Den Auftrag für diesen Kulturbau, der Roland Rainers monumental sich aufbäumende Wiener Stadthalle ergänzt, hatten sie sich in einem internationalen Wettbewerb gesichert. Das schnittige, vielfach geknickte Gebäude spiegelt mit seinen grossen verglasten Foyers Rainers Nachkriegsikone und bestimmt als dialogfähige

project is completely derived from the topography of the slope, to which we responded with a system of quadrangles, triangles and parallelograms." (D)
But not all Swiss competition projects were successful. For instance their proposals for the redesign of Roschach harbour in 2003, the new casino in Basel and the transformation of the *Theater 11* in Zurich only achieved unrewarding second or third places. Yet the expansively projecting volume for the *Theater 11* could have become an attractive flagship for Zurich's Oerlikon urban quarter, since the design, which bears a faint resemblance to Rem Koolhaas' Casa da Música in Porto, oscillates between Minimalism and Baroque; it represents an unconventional further development of Hall F of the *Wiener Stadthalle* music and event centre, which was conceived in 2002 and completed in 2005.
The order for that cultural building, which supplements Roland Rainer's monumentally rearing *Wiener Stadthalle*, was the result of winning another international competition. The streamlined building with many folds reflects Rainer's post-war icon with its large glazed foyer and defines the square and street space along Hütteldorfer Strasse as an interactive urban planning figure in the form of a hexagon that is slightly compressed in its ground plan and elevation. "We produced a functional and formal connection. You owe that much to the prominent neighbouring building by Roland Rainer. The new hall now stands very simply and naturally in its position."[2]

Schulgebäude/School building, Klaus, 2003

städtebauliche Figur in Form eines in Grund- und Aufriss leicht gestauchten Sechsecks den Platz- und Strassenraum an der Hütteldorfer Strasse. «Wir haben funktional und formal einen Konnex hergestellt, soviel ist man dem prominenten Nachbarbau von Roland Rainer schuldig. Die neue Halle steht jetzt ganz simpel und selbstverständlich da.»[2]

Nach dem Wiener Wettbewerb beteiligten sich Dietrich|Untertrifaller an weiteren prestigeträchtigen Auslobungen für das Olympic Village *2012* in New York (2003), für die IUCN-Erweiterung in Genf (2005), für die norwegische Neustadt Siriskjaer bei Stavanger (2006) und für das Krakauer Kongresszentrum (2007), aber sie wurden mit keinem Auftrag belohnt. Dafür konnten sie 2007 die zusammen mit Roland Gnaiger konzipierte Reka-Siedlung in Urnäsch vollenden – gleichsam als ländlich-bescheidene Antithese zur grossstädtisch-selbstbewussten Wiener Musik- und Veranstaltungshalle F. Mit der Urnäscher Ferienanlage bewiesen Dietrich|Untertrifaller, dass in ihrem Œuvre neben polygonal-neokubistischen, wie Kristalle geschliffenen Bauten – zu denen beispielsweise die 2011 übergebene Blockrandbebauung in Aarau gezählt werden kann – weiterhin auch «einfache, pragmatische Holzhäuser» (D) eine Rolle spielen.

In dem malerischen, von schönen Giebelhäusern geprägten Appenzeller-Dorf entschieden sie sich – anders als etwa bei den Einfamilienhäusern im Bregenzerwald – für Flachdachbauten. «Obwohl Flachdächer in Urnäsch nicht selbstverständlich sind, konnten wir die Bevölkerung davon überzeugen, dass Häuser auch so aussehen dürfen.» (D) Mit der kammartigen Anlage, die sich entschieden vom alten Dorfkern abhebt, wagten sie es, einen harten, von «klarer Geometrie und fast schon simpler Reihung» (D) geprägten Akzent in die harmonische Landschaft zu setzen. An den vierfach abgetreppten, sich der Strasse entlang ziehenden Gemeinschaftsbau fügen sich drei nach Norden abgewinkelte Baukörper mit insgesamt 50 Ferienwohnungen an. «Hier den dörflichen Massstab oder denjenigen der Gehöfte aufzunehmen, schlossen wir bewusst aus. Denn wir hätten den wunderbar kompakten Dorfkern eher geschwächt, wenn wir in der gleichen Art weitergebaut hätten. So sehen wir denn die Anlage als eine Art gebaute Landschaft, die eher Teil der Topografie als Teil des Dorfes ist.» (D)

Nachhaltigkeit und Ökologie

Neben den Grossaufträgen von Wien und Urnäsch widmeten sich Dietrich|Untertrifaller weiterhin auch kleineren Arbeiten. Denn ebenso wie die aufsehenerregende Form liegt ihnen die baumeisterliche Präzision, bei deren Umsetzung sie sich auf die hohen handwerklichen Standards in Vorarlberg verlassen

Following the Vienna competition, Dietrich|Untertrifaller participated in further prestigious tender invitations for the 2012 Olympic Village in New York (2003), the IUCN extension in Geneva (2005), the Norwegian new town Siriskjaer near Stavanger (2006) and the Cracow Congress Centre (2007), although none of these won contracts. However in 2007, they joined forces with Roland Gnaiger to design the Reka estate in Urnäsch and were able to complete it – also as a modest, rural antithesis to the metropolitan, confident Hall F in Vienna. The Urnäsch holiday camp proves how "simple, pragmatic wooden houses" (D) also play a role in their work, in addition to polygonal, Neocubist buildings that are polished like crystals – which include the block perimeter development in Aarau that was completed in 2011.

In the picturesque Appenzell village that is characterised by fine gabled houses, they decided on a different approach compared to their single-family homes in Bregenz Forest – choosing flat roofed buildings. "Although flat roofs are not a matter of course in Urnäsch, we were able to convince the local residents that houses can also look like that." (D) The ridge-like camp, which distinguishes itself strongly from the old village centre, was a daring attempt to add a hard accent to the harmonious landscape, one that was characterised by, "clear geometry and almost simple rows." (D) Three buildings with a total of 50 holiday apartments are angled northwards from the four-fold staggered communal building that stretches along the road. "We deliberately decided against assuming the scale of the village or farms. In doing so, we would have weakened the wonderfully compact village centre by continuing to build in the same way. So we regard the camp as a kind of constructed landscape, which is more part of the topography than of the village." (D)

Sustainability and Ecology

In addition to major contracts such as those in Vienna and Urnäsch, Dietrich|Untertrifaller continue to work on smaller projects. Because they are equally skilled in masterbuilding precision as they are in high-profile forms, since in implementing the former, they can rely on the high standards of craftsmanship in the Vorarlberg region. A good example of this is the Angelika Kauffmann Museum in Schwarzenberg, which was inaugurated in 2007, and for which artistic carpentry and state of the art steel construction techniques went hand in hand. The modern wooden architecture consisting of a foyer and a museum hall was integrated into the utility wing of one of the most beautiful farmhouses in Bregenz Forest, which has accommodated a museum of local history in its residential section for a long time. While the actual exhibition area of

Einkaufsmarkt/Hypermarket, Eurospar Vorkloster, Bregenz, 2006

Wettbewerb/Competition, Stadthof 11 (Stadttheater/City theatre), Zürich, 2003

Wohnhaus/Apartment building Lineaar, Aarau, 2011

Haus/House A, Dornbirn, 2009

Haus/House R, Schnepfau, 1998

Haus/House K, Schwarzenberg, 2003

Haus/House S, Egg, 1998

Haus/House R, Bregenz, 2002

können. Exemplarisch mag dafür das 2007 eingeweihte Angelika-Kauffmann-Museum in Schwarzenberg stehen, bei dem kunstvolle Schreinerarbeit und neueste Stahlbautechnik harmonisch zusammenfinden. Integriert wurde die moderne Holzarchitektur von Foyer und Museumsraum in den Wirtschaftstrakt eines der schönsten Bregenzerwälder Bauernhäuser, dessen Wohnteil schon seit geraumer Zeit als Heimatmuseum dient. Während der eigentliche Ausstellungssaal des Angelika-Kauffmann-Museums aus einem klar von den Scheunenwänden abgesetzten Volumen besteht, treten im Foyer die neuen Einbauten mit der alten Wand des Bauernhauses und dem historischen Dachstuhl in einen Dialog.

Ging es bei diesem Umbau nicht zuletzt auch um die Auseinandersetzung mit der Baukultur des Bregenzerwaldes, so holen die ganz in der Tradition der alemannischen Streusiedlungen am Sonnenhang oder in aussichtsreicher Höhe platzierten Einfamilienhäuser und Villen – ganz ähnlich wie die Bauten in Zürich oder Urnäsch – ihre Kraft aus der Topografie. «Die Topografie ist in unserer Entwurfsarbeit wichtiger als die bauliche Umgebung. Geländeveränderungen gibt es bei uns selten. Wenn wir am Hang bauen, dann bleibt der Hang bestehen. Ebenso wichtig wie die Landschaft sind uns aber auch die Menschen. Das zeigt sich etwa beim Haus A oberhalb von Dornbirn.» (D) Der in neuester Holzbautechnik ausgeführte Bau steht mit seinen schönen Proportionen und logischen Grundrissen in einer Entwicklungslinie, die über die Häuser Rüscher in Schnepfau und Kaufmann in Schwarzenberg zurückreicht bis zum 1998 in Egg errichteten Haus Sutterlüty.

Das Büro Dietrich|Untertrifaller baut aber nicht nur solch erdverbundene Einfamilienhäuser. Von ihm stammen auch einige exzentrischere Werke wie die am Bregenzer Pfänder-Abhang, der österreichischen Riviera, sich in einem Swimmingpool spiegelnde Villa Rhomberg (2002), das in den Wiesen hoch über Dornbirn auf einem Betonsockel balancierende «Haus am Hang» oder die L-förmig komponierte, hollywoodesk anmutende Villa LK in Hard (2009). Ausser diesen Vorzeigebauten sind seit dem Jahr 2000 noch etwa 50 weitere Einfamilienhäuser und Villen sowie rund 35 architektonisch weniger prätentiöse, urbanistisch aber wichtige Wohnanlagen und Mehrfamilienhäuser entstanden. Hervorgehoben werden soll hier die zwischen 2004 und 2006 aus vier fünfgeschossigen Bauten errichtete Öko-Siedlung Mühlweg in Wien Floridsdorf, deren Holzkonstruktionen aus Brandschutzgründen mit Gipsfaserplatten verkleidet werden mussten. «Unkonventionelle Lösungen wie in der Schweiz sind bei uns kaum möglich. Denn die Wohnungsgrundrisse sind knapp. Bei uns misst eine 3,5-Zimmer-Wohnung

the Angelika Kauffmann Museum consists of a volume that is clearly set apart from the barn walls, the new buildings enter into a dialogue with the old farmhouse wall and the historical roof truss in the foyer.

While this conversion was not least a study of the building culture of Bregenz Forest, the single family homes and villas, which are clearly in the tradition of Alemannic scattered, sunny-slope settlements, or are positioned at promising heights, draw their strength from the topography – in a very similar way to the buildings in Zurich or Urnäsch. "The topography is more important to our design work than the built environment. We rarely change the terrain. If we build on a slope, the slope remains. But people are just as important to us as the landscape. You can see that for instance in *Haus A* above Dornbirn." (D) The building, which has been constructed using state of the art wooden building methods and has beautiful proportions with logical ground plans, is part of a line of development that spans the Rüscher houses in Schnepfau, the Kaufmann house in Schwarzenburg and the *Haus Sutterlüty* constructed in Egg in 1998.

But Dietrich|Untertrifaller do not only build such earth-bound single-family homes. They have also produced a number of eccentric works, for instance the Villa Rhomberg (2002) with its swimming-pool reflection, on the slopes of the Pfänder mountain, the Austrian Riviera. Other examples are the *Haus am Hang* that balances on a concrete base in the meadows high above Dornbirn, as well as the L-shaped design of the Hollywoodesque Villa LK in Hard (2009). In addition to those prominent buildings, around another 50 single-family homes and villas, as well as around 35 less architecturally ostentatious, urban, yet important residential estates and apartment buildings have been built since 2000. Worthy of special note is the *Öko-Siedlung Mühlweg* in Vienna Floridsdorf that was built between 2004 and 2006, consisting of four five-storey buildings. Its wooden structures had to be clad in fibreboard for fire protection reasons. "Unconventional solutions like those in Switzerland are hardly possible for us. Apartment floor space is limited. Our 3.5-room apartments have 70 m^2, compared to 100 m^2 in Switzerland. So there's only leeway for designing the façade and the access area." (D)

Unlike the Vienna Mühlweg estate, the extension to the Holztechnikum Kuchl, which is part of the Salzburg University of Applied Sciences, presents its wooden structure with no cladding on the inside or outside. The extension, which can be accessed from the old school building via a three-storey connecting structure, provides a foyer, an art room that can be used for events, a library, a photo studio and five

70 Quadratmeter, in der Schweiz rund 100 Quadratmeter. Spielraum gibt es nur bei der Fassadengestaltung und der Erschliessung.» (D)
Anders als die Wiener Siedlung Mühlweg darf der Erweiterungsbau des zur Fachhochschule Salzburg gehörenden Holztechnikums in Kuchl seine Holzkonstruktion nach innen und aussen unverhüllt zur Schau stellen. Der vom alten Schulgebäude aus über einen dreigeschossigen Verbindungsgang zugängliche Anbau bietet neben einem Foyer und dem als Veranstaltungsraum nutzbaren Zeichensaal eine Bibliothek, ein Fotostudio und fünf Seminarräume. Während die südseitige Front als tragende Holzwand ausgebildet ist, schützen an der Ost- und an der Westfassade angebrachte horizontale Holzlamellen die Innenräume vor Sonnenlicht – ganz ähnlich wie die Kupfertrapezbleche bei der Hauptschule in Klaus. Dieser erste in moderner Holzbau- und Passivhaustechnik errichtete Hochschulbau Österreichs dient den Studierenden in Kuchl täglich als Best-Practice-Beispiel. «Ökologisches Bauen sollte schon längst selbstverständlich sein. Es ist doch unbestritten, dass Ökologie in einer modernen Hülle Platz haben kann.»[3]
Im Büro Dietrich|Untertrifaller wird jedoch nicht nur über Ökologie und Nachhaltigkeit, sondern auch über Material, Typologie und Topografie diskutiert. «Aber wir schreiben diese Erkenntnisse nicht als Regulativ für unser Schaffen nieder.» (D) Obwohl es durchaus Entwurfsmaximen gibt, befassten sich die Bregenzer Architekten nie eingehender mit Theorie. «Das hängt vielleicht damit zusammen, dass unser Büro von Anfang an vollbeschäftigt war und wir nie die Musse hatten, über theoretische Fragen nachzudenken.» (U)
Zu den Themen, die sie immer wieder beschäftigen, zählt auch die Angemessenheit: «Wir versuchen bei jeder Bauaufgabe, einen angemessenen Ausdruck, eine angemessene Form zu finden. Das kann sehr unterschiedlich ausfallen. Beim Einfamilienhaus ist das meistens die zurückgenommene Form, die auch etwas mit der jeweiligen lokalen Tradition zu tun hat. Beim Festspielhaus ist es die Angemessenheit eines bedeutenden Gebäudes im öffentlichen Raum.» (D)

Städtebauliche Ansätze

Das Bregenzer Festspielhaus ist aber nicht nur als kulturelles Monument von Interesse, sondern auch als eine vielschichtige Stadt im Kleinen. Dieser urbanistische Aspekt lässt sich aus dem additiven Entwurfsprinzip erklären, aber auch damit, dass städtebauliche Überlegungen bereits früh das Schaffen von Dietrich|Untertrifaller bestimmten. Angesichts der rasant fortschreitenden Zersiedlung der sich von Lochau bis Feldkirch erstreckenden Vorarlberger Bandstadt *Rheintal* ist ihnen die Neugestaltung und Verdichtung

seminar rooms. While the south-facing front is designed as a load-bearing wooden wall, horizontal slats protect the interior from the sunlight on the eastern and western façades – in a very similar way to the copper sheet metal in the Klaus secondary school. It is the first university building in Austria to have been built using modern wood construction methods that conform to passive house standards. Every day, it serves as a best-practice example to students in Kuchl. "Ecological building should long be considered as a matter of course. It's undisputed that there is space for ecology in a modern shell."[3]
However Dietrich|Untertrifaller not only discuss ecology and sustainability, but also materials, typology and topography. "But we don't prescribe that insight as a regulator for our work." (D) Although there certainly are design maxims, the Bregenz architects have never studied theory in depth. "That is perhaps because our office always worked to capacity and we never had the time to consider theoretical matters." (U)
One theme that they constantly work on is appropriateness: "In every building project, we try to find an appropriate expression, an appropriate form. That can lead to very different results. In the case of a single-family home for instance, it means a reserved form that also has something to do with the relevant local tradition. A festival hall requires the appropriateness of an important public building." (D)

Urban planning approaches

The Bregenz Festival House is not only interesting as a cultural monument, but also as a miniature, multilayered city. That urban aspect can be explained by the additive design principle Dietrich|Untertrifaller apply and also by the fact that urban planning considerations determine their work at an early stage. In view of the rapid growth of settlements in the Vorarlberg linear city "Rheintal", the restructuring and densification of historically developed centres is very important to them. Even at the start of their careers, theiy built two Y-shaped, mutually referential buildings in Hofsteigstrasse in Hard, picking up on the alignment of the neighbouring buildings on a public square that is framed by shops. Their measures affecting the urban landscape of Bregenz reflects the larger scale there. Dietrich|Untertrifaller responded to the Kunsthaus, with which Peter Zumthor had continued to weave the urban texture of the lakeside suburb in 1997, by creating the commercial and residential complex "Am Hafen", which was constructed between 2002 and 2005 in an exposed location at the northern entrance to the town centre.
In that project, they convincingly extended the urban grain of the lakeside suburb, which is framed by the

Haus/House LK, Hard, 2009

[3] Vgl. Anm. 2.

[3] Cf. footnote 2.

Öko-Wohnsiedlung/Ecological housing complex Mühlweg, Wien, 2006

Erweiterung/Extension Fachhochschule Salzburg, Kuchl, 2009

Geschäfts- und Wohnkomplex/
Business and apartment complex Am Hafen, Bregenz, 2005

Bürogebäude/Business building
Office am See, Bregenz, 2006

Wohngebäude/Apartment building
Belruptstrasse,
Bregenz, 2008

historisch gewachsener Zentren ein Anliegen. So realisierten sie schon zu Beginn ihrer Karriere an der Hofsteigstrasse in Hard mit zwei y-förmig aufeinander bezogenen Baukörpern, die die Ausrichtung der Nachbarbauten aufnehmen, einen von Geschäften gefassten öffentlichen Platz. Einem grösseren Massstab verpflichtet sind ihre Eingriffe ins Stadtgefüge von Bregenz. Auf das Kunsthaus, mit dem Peter Zumthor bereits 1997 die urbanistische Textur der Seevorstadt weiterwebte, antworteten Dietrich|Untertrifaller mit dem zwischen 2002 und 2005 in exponierter Lage am Nordeingang zum Stadtzentrum realisierten Geschäfts- und Wohnkomplex *Am Hafen*.
Bei diesem Projekt setzten sie die urbanistische Körnung der von Bahnlinie und Strasse begrenzten Seevorstadt überzeugend fort, mit einem siebengeschossigen Büroturm und drei kammartig über einem verglasten Sockel angeordneten fünfgeschossigen Wohnriegeln, von deren Balkonen aus man einen Traumblick auf den Bodensee hat. Der Sockelbau rahmt die Ausfallstrasse und spielt mit städtebaulicher Präzision vor dem Hochhaus an der Strassenkreuzung einen Platz frei. «Hier reizte uns der Versuch, einen Eckpfeiler der Stadt zu schaffen. Die Höhe des Hochhauses gab Anlass zu Diskussionen. Doch wir konnten darauf hinweisen, dass es die vertikalen Akzente von Post, Kunsthaus und Theater fortsetzt.» (D) Zu diesen vertikalen Akzenten gesellte sich kurz darauf das einige Hundert Meter weiter südlich an der Uferstrasse gelegene *Office am See*, das mit einem sechsgeschossigen Turm und zwei niedrigeren Verbindungsbauten geschickt auf die städtebauliche Situation eingeht und zwischen zwei architektonischen Grössenordnungen vermittelt.
Auch im eigentlichen Stadtkern von Bregenz vermochten Dietrich|Untertrifaller immer wieder mit kleinen, urbanistisch und architektonisch gleichermassen subtilen Eingriffen zu brillieren. Bereits 1997 ergänzten sie einen Blockrand mit einem zur Schillerstrasse hin kompakten, zum Hof hin aber in grosse, loggienartige Balkone aufgelösten fünfgeschossigen Wohnhaus, das sie an ein repräsentatives ehemaliges Molkereigebäude von Willibald Braun andockten. Sieben Jahre später konnten sie einen Blockrand an der Belruptstrasse mit dem Bürgerhaus schliessen, dessen neuklassizistisch-minimalistische, durch stehende Lochfenster geprägte Fassade eine städtebaulich wichtige Ecksituation stärkt.
Weniger erdenschwer gibt sich der mondän über einem verglasten Erdgeschoss schwebende Anbau an den 1921 ebenfalls von Willibald Braun errichteten, durch ionische Halbsäulen nobilitierten ehemaligen Sitz des Vorarlberger Landtags, der in den 1980er Jahren in ein Bürohaus verwandelt und um

train track and the street, to add a seven-storey office tower and three five-storey residential blocks that are aligned like a comb on a glazed base, with balconies that provide a wonderful view of Lake Constance. The plinthed building frames the arterial road and uses urban planning precision to create an open space at the road junction in front of the high-rise building. "We were keen to try to create a cornerstone for the city. The height of the high-rise building was a cause of debate. But we were able to show that it complemented the vertical accents of the post office, the *Kunsthaus* and the theatre." (D) Shortly afterwards, these vertical accents were joined by the *Office am See* ("Office by the Lake") on the waterfront road a few hundred metres further south. It is a six-storey tower with two low connecting buildings that cleverly interacts with the urban planning situation, mediating between two architectural scales.
In the actual centre of Bregenz, Dietrich|Untertrifaller have also regularly impressed with small, urban architectural measures that are equally subtle. As early as in 1997, they created a five-storey residential block perimeter building that was compact towards Schillerstrasse, but is dispersed towards the inner courtyard through large, loggia-like balconies. It is docked onto a prestigious former dairy building designed by Willibald Braun. Seven years later, they closed a gap in the perimeter development along Belruptstrasse with the *Bürgerhaus*. Its Neoclassicist-Minimalist façade is characterised by casement windows to enhance a corner situation with urban planning significance.
Another building by Willibald Braun was the seat of the Voarlberg Parliament, which was constructed in 1921 and is ennobled by ionic half-pedestals, before being converted into an office building in the 1980s and extended to include a postmodern annexe. This extension is less heavy than the building in Belruptstrasse, since it hovers above a glazed ground floor. Dietrich|Untertrifaller had the task of converting it into the Hypo-Bank headquarters. They reacted to the horizontally accentuating effect of the façades of the completely redesigned extension on the vertical rhythm of the temple-like building and clarified the transition from old to new through glass joints.
While Dietrich|Untertrifaller were working to drive the Hypo-Bank project forward and also converting the Bregenz Velag estate to create an inviting residential development consisting of old industrial buildings and two new houses, they were also eagerly anticipating the result of the vote on their freight railway station project in St. Gallen, which was announced in June 2007. Without doubt, it was their most complex urban planning project to date, since it converted a historical freight hall and composed

einen postmodernen Annex erweitert wurde. Diesen bauten Dietrich|Untertrifaller nun zur Hypobank-Zentrale um. Dabei antworteten sie mit den die Horizontale akzentuierenden Fassaden des völlig umgestalteten Erweiterungsbaus auf den vertikalen Rhythmus des tempelartigen Hauptgebäudes und klärten den Übergang von Alt und Neu mit gläsernen Fugen. Während Dietrich|Untertrifaller die Realisierung der Hypobank-Zentrale vorantrieben und am Umbau des Bregenzer Velag-Areals in eine einladende, aus alten Fabrikgebäuden und zwei neuen Häusern bestehende Wohnanlage arbeiteten, fieberten sie im Juni 2007 dem Ausgang der Abstimmung über ihr Güterbahnhof-Projekt in St. Gallen entgegen. Denn das aus einer historischen Frachthalle, zwei lang gestreckten, blitzartig gezackten Neubauten und zwei diese fassenden acht- und zwölfgeschossigen Hochhäusern komponierte Quartier zwischen Bahnlinie und Berghang war zweifellos die bis dahin städtebaulich komplexeste Arbeit des Büros. Doch die St. Galler Stimmbürger verwehrten dem grossstädtischen Entwurf ihre Zustimmung – was sich längst als verpasste Chance erwiesen hat. Erfolgreicher waren sie hingegen beim Wettbewerb für die Neugestaltung des Bahnhofsviertels in Bregenz. Zwar wurde ihr Projekt nicht mit dem ersten Preis ausgezeichnet. «Dafür machen wir den Bahnhof neu und das Hochhaus am Bahnhof, den Bahnhofsplatz und die Strassengestaltung.» (U) Hier werden sie einmal mehr beweisen können, dass sie «für die Stadt hochwertige Orchesterarbeit leisten und auf dem Land sensibel erfühlte Kammermusik».[4]

Bauen in Deutschland und Frankreich

Auch wenn derzeit eine junge Garde versucht, die regionale Szene aufzumischen, bleibt die Anzahl grosser Bauaufgaben in Vorarlberg beschränkt. Deshalb haben Dietrich|Untertrifaller sich vermehrt auf internationale Aufträge spezialisiert: in Deutschland, der Schweiz – und vor allem auch in Frankreich. «Wir glauben, dass das Vorarlberger Modell derzeit von aussen wieder sehr stark wahrgenommen wird. Weniger vielleicht von Architekten und Bauherren, die sich in einem urbanen Kontext bewegen, als vielmehr von Vertretern von Regionen, die ähnliche Probleme und Zielsetzungen haben wie Vorarlberg. Und die lauten: aus einer nicht urbanen, ländlichen Situation heraus ein modernes Land zu schaffen. Deswegen schauen gerade die Franzosen interessiert nach Vorarlberg, denn bei ihnen sind die Probleme der Provinz noch viel ausgeprägter als bei uns.» (D)
Das Frankreich-Abenteuer von Dietrich|Untertrifaller begann mit dem Bauauftrag für die neue École Nationale Supérieure d'Art in Nancy, den sie sich 2010

two elongated, lightning-bolt shaped new buildings and two framing high-rise buildings, with eight and twelve storeys respectively, on the estate between the train tracks and hillside. But the St. Gallen voters rejected the metropolitan design. It has long been clear that this was a missed opportunity. However they were more successful with the new design for the Bregenz station quarter. Their project did not win 1st prize, "But we renewed the station and the high-rise building at the station, the station square and the street design." (U) It will give them a chance to prove again that they, "can provide the city with high-quality orchestral work and gentle chamber music for the countryside." [4]

Building in Germany and France

Even though a wave of young architects is currently attempting to stir up the regional scene, the number of major construction tasks in Vorarlberg is limited. So Dietrich|Untertrifaller have increasingly specialised in international contracts: in Germany, Switzerland and especially in France. "We believe that the Vorarlberg model is again attracting great attention from abroad. Perhaps less by architects and builders who move in an urban context, but certainly by representatives of regions that have similar problems and aims to those in Vorarlberg. And they are: to create a modern country out of a non-urban, rural situation. So the French are especially interested in Vorarlberg, since their provincial problems are much more serious than ours." (D)

Wohngebäude/Apartment building
Schillerstrasse, Bregenz, 1997

[4] Otto Kapfinger am 20. Januar 2010 in seiner Rede zur Eröffnung der Ausstellung Dietrich|Untertrifaller im Zumtobel Lichtforum in Wien.

[4] Otto Kapfinger on January 20, 2010 in his speech at the opening of the exhibition on Dietrich|Untertrifaller in the Zumtobel Lichtforum, Vienna

Geschäftsgebäude/Business building
Hypobank-Zentrale, Bregenz, 2008

Wettbewerb/Competition Güterbahnhof/Freight railway station, St. Gallen, 2005 (1. Preis/1st Prize)

Überbauung/Building complex Seequartier, Bregenz (in Planung/in Planning)

Schulgebäude/School building École Nationale Supérieure d'Art, Nancy (in Planung/in planning)

Konzerthaus/Concert hall Palais de la Musique et des Congrès, Strassburg (in Planung/in planning)

zusammen mit dem französischen Büro Zoméno in einem Wettbewerb sichern konnten. Der Neubau soll aus zwei einen Hof umfassenden Baukörpern – einem orthogonalen Längsbau und einem mehrfach abgewinkelten Kubus – bestehen und bis 2014 auf einem ehemaligen, nun als Universitätscampus dienenden Kasernenareal errichtet werden. «Wir sind bewusst strategisch nach Frankreich gegangen. Anfangs haben uns französische Büros kontaktiert; doch wir haben das nicht sehr ernst genommen. Seit Nancy aber liegt die Initiative bei uns, weil wir erkannt haben, dass das Wettbewerbswesen in Frankreich für uns sehr interessant ist.» (U)
Volumen- und prestigemässig noch bedeutender als die Kunsthochschule von Nancy ist zweifellos die Sanierung und Erweiterung des Palais de la Musique et des Congrès in Strassburg. Mit ihrem Projekt, das auf dem Erfahrungsschatz von Bregenz und Wien basiert, konnten sie 2011 in einem internationalen Ausschreiben namhafte Büros wie Sauerbruch Hutton und Ben van Berkels UN-Studio ausstechen. Neben dem Umbau der beiden bestehenden Musiksäle schlagen sie den Bau eines käferförmigen Konferenzsaals, eines Übungssaals und eines Foyers vor, das die drei Bereiche Konzert, Kongress und Ausstellung vereint und erschliesst. Dabei halten sie am ursprünglichen, auf Drei- und Sechsecken basierenden Formenvokabular der Altbauten fest, doch wollen sie dem gesamten Komplex mit einer neuen, zwischen Säulenhalle und Vorhang oszillierenden Hülle ein einheitliches Erscheinungsbild verleihen. «Diese fast einen Kilometer lange Kolonnade ist deshalb wichtig, weil die bestehenden Bauteile so unterschiedlich und so schlecht sind, dass sie mit ihren Fassaden einfach nicht bestehen können. Daher ziehen wir hier – anders als beim Festspielhaus in Bregenz mit seinen ablesbaren Teilen – eine einheitliche Hülle um den Baukomplex herum.» (U)
Dietrich|Untertrifaller gehen davon aus, dass sie in Nancy und Strassburg hinsichtlich ihres Detailbewusstseins Abstriche machen und «eine andere Ästhetik entwickeln werden müssen, damit das Ergebnis stimmig wird. In Frankreich baut man unter anderen Voraussetzungen als in Vorarlberg. Denn Frankreich ist kein Land der Handwerker, sondern eine Industrienation.» (U) Inzwischen haben Dietrich|Untertrifaller in Frankreich zwei weitere wichtige Wettbewerbe gewonnen: für eine Sporthalle in Longvic bei Dijon und für ein grosses regionales Collège in Broons, einem kleinen Dorf bei Rennes in der Bretagne.
Auch in Deutschland sind bedeutende Neubauten im Bau oder in Planung. Während ihr Projekt eines Kongress- und Konzertgebäudes mit Freiluftbühne in Konstanz an den politischen Hürden scheiterte,

The French adventure for Dietrich|Untertrifaller began with the construction order for the new École Nationale Supérieure d'Art in Nancy, for which they won the competition in 2010 with a joint entry together with the French office Zoméno. The new building will consist of two volumes surrounding a courtyard: an orthogonal, long building and one cuboid that is angled several times. It will be erected by 2014 on a former barracks that now serves as a university campus. "It was a conscious strategic decision to go to France. We were initially contacted by French offices, but didn't take that very seriously. But since Nancy, the initiative has been from us. We realised that the competition scene in France is a very exciting field for us." (U)
In terms of volume and prestige, the renovation and extension of the Palais de la Musique et des Congrès in Strassburg is even more significant than the art school in Nancy. Their 2011 project, which is based on their wealth of experience from Bregenz and Vienna, allowed them to overcome renowned competitors such as Sauerbruch Hutton and Ben van Berkel's UN-Studio. In addition to converting the two existing music halls, they propose the construction of a beetle-shaped conference hall, a rehearsal room and a foyer that unifies and connects the three fields of concerts, congresses and exhibitions. In doing so, they stick to the original formal vocabulary of the existing buildings, which is based on triangles and hexagons, while nevertheless wishing to give the entire complex a unified appearance through the addition of a new shell that oscillates between a hall of columns and a curtain. "This almost one kilometre long colonnade is important because existing building elements vary so greatly and are so poor that they simply cannot remain with their façades. That's why unlike the Festival House in Bregenz, with its legible parts – we shrouded this building complex with a uniform shell (U)."
Dietrich|Untertrifaller presume that in Nancy and Strasbourg, they will have to make compromises with respect to their attention to detail and, "develop a different kind of aesthetics to come to a coherent result. Construction work in France has different preconceptions to those in Vorarlberg. France is not a country of craftsmen and is instead an industrial nation." (U) Since then, Dietrich|Untertrifaller have won two other important competitions in France: for the sports hall in Longvic near Dijon and for a large regional college in Broons, a small village near Rennes in Brittany.
In Germany too, major new buildings are either currently under construction or in planning. While their project for a congress and concert centre with

konnte ihre Erweiterung der Grundschule in Frankfurt-Kalbach unlängst eingeweiht werden. «Derzeit arbeiten wir – ausgehend von gewonnenen Wettbewerben – an einem weitläufigen Büroquartier auf dem Gelände der Kokerei Zollverein in Essen und an der aus fünf Atriumhäusern und drei Dreispännern bestehenden Siedlung Am Nonnensteg in Göttingen. Von Daimler Benz wurden wir zu einem Wettbewerb für ein Future Center eingeladen, das neben dem Mercedes-Benz Museum von Ben van Berkel in Stuttgart entstehen soll; und in Dresden nehmen wir an einer Ausschreibung für ein Musiktheater teil.» (D)
Im Zusammenhang mit all ihren Bauten und Projekten betonen Helmut Dietrich und Much Untertrifaller immer wieder, wie wichtig ihnen der Umgang mit dem Vorgefundenen, mit der Topografie, dem Ort und dem Kontext ist. «Unser Erfolg rührt aber vielleicht auch daher, dass wir uns immer wieder zur richtigen Zeit mit den richtigen Themen beschäftigt haben. Auf Holzbau und Nachhaltigkeit haben wir bereits zu einer Zeit gesetzt, als viele unserer Kollegen noch der Ansicht waren, diese Aufgaben würden ihre Kreativität zu sehr einschränken.» (D) Früh schon konnten sie beweisen, dass energieeffiziente Architektur nicht schwerfällig sein muss. «Das öffnete uns sehr viele Türen. Auch heute scheuen wir uns nicht vor neuen Herausforderungen.» (U) So sind immer wieder von Weitsicht und Augenmass geprägte Bauten entstanden, die nie in die seichte Oberflächlichkeit der internationalen Stararchitektur abgleiten. Dies nicht zuletzt aufgrund der Tatsache, dass die beiden Architekten sich in der Entwurfsarbeit gut ergänzen, «weil Much keine Angst vor dem grossen Massstab und der grossen Aufgabe hat und ich vielleicht stärker im Detail und im kleinen Massstab die Dinge vorantreibe. Das ist heute selten, da die meisten Architekten entweder im Detail stecken bleiben oder sich nur noch mit Konzepten beschäftigen.» (D)

an open-air stage in Constance failed to overcome political obstacles, their extension for the primary school in Frankfurt-Kalbach was recently officially opened. "Based on the competitions we've won, we're currently working on an extensive office quarter on the estate of the *Kokerei Zollverein* in Essen and on the *Am Nonnensteg* settlement in Göttingen, consisting of five atrium houses and three triple-apartments. We were invited by Daimler Benz to participate in a competition for a Future Center that is planned beside the Mercedes-Benz Museum designed by Ben van Berkel in Stuttgart. And in Dresden we're taking part in a competition for a musical theatre." (D)
In connection with all their buildings and projects, Helmut Dietrich and Much Untertrifaller constantly stress how important they find the way one treats what already exists, the topography, the location and the context. "But perhaps our success is also based on the fact that we have repeatedly focused on the right themes at the right time. We already focused on wooden construction and sustainability at a time when many of our colleagues still believed that such consideration would inhibit their creativity too much." (D) But in fact they were able to prove at an early stage that energy-efficient architecture does not need to be cumbersome. "That opened a great many doors for us. Even today, we don't shy away from new challenges." (U) In that way, they have regularly produced buildings that are characterised by farsightedness and a sense of proportion, while never sliding into the shallow superficiality of international star architecture. That is not least due to the fact that the two architects complement each other so well in their design work, "because Much is not afraid of large scales and great tasks, while I perhaps work more keenly on details and smaller scales. That's rare nowadays, since most architects either get stuck in details or only work on concepts." (D)

Sportzentrum/Sports centre, Longvic
(in Planung/in planning)

Schulgebäude/School building Collège
Jean Monnet, Broons F (in Planung/in planning)

Schulgebäude/School building
Grundschule Kalbach, Frankfurt, 2012

Neubaugürtel/Band of new developement
Kokerei Zollverein, Essen

Festspielhaus, Bregenz

Bregenz Festival House

Wettbewerb/Competition: 1992
Ausführung/Construction: 2005–2006; 1995–1997
Bauherr/Client: Stadt Bregenz, Land Vorarlberg, Republik Österreich
Planung/Planning: Dietrich|Untertrifaller
Projektleitung/Project management: S. Gaudl, H. Walker (2006), A. Rüf (1997)
Auszeichnungen/Awards: 2010 *Apex-Award*; 2007 *Int. Architecture Award*

Partner:
Statik/Statics: Mader Flatz Plankel, Bregenz; Haustechnik/Service engineers: Pfügl Roth, Bregenz; Elektro-Akustik/Electro-acoustics: Tonplan, Dornbirn; Bühnentechnik/Stage engineers: Kottke, Bayreuth; Akustik/Acoustics: Müller BBM, Planegg; Licht/Lighting: Keller, St. Gallen; Landschaftsarchitektur/Landscape architecture: Vogt, Zürich

Architektur als Bühne

Wie eine Stadt im Kleinen konzipierten Dietrich|Untertrifaller die Grundrisse des aus einem 1992 durchgeführten Wettbewerb hervorgegangenen neuen Festspielhauses in Bregenz. In zwei Etappen verwandelten sie das alte, 1980 direkt am Bodensee eröffnete Theater von Wilhelm Braun mittels einer Collage unterschiedlicher Bauteile sowie neugeschaffener interner Erschliessungsachsen in ein skulptural anmutendes Gebäude. Südlich des Altbaus errichteten sie eine Werkstattbühne und setzten gleichzeitig mit dem als Riegel über beide Bauteile gelegten Verbindungs- und Verwaltungstrakt einen starken Akzent. Diesem antwortet seit 2006 eine zweite durchgesteckte Spange, die als Besucherbereich auf niedrigerer Ebene das Haus durchstösst und im seeseitigen Foyer endet. Die öffentliche und die interne Erschliessungszone überlagern sich bei den Liften und dienen so auch der Logistik des Festspielhauses. Das bald kubisch verschlossene, bald durch grosse Fensterflächen belebte Gebäude rahmt die auf 6800 Sitzplätze erweiterte Seebühne und verfügt nun über einen 1800 Zuschauer fassenden Theatersaal sowie ein Seestudio. Dazu kommen das Restaurant, elegante Foyers und der doppelgeschossig auf den weiten Vorplatz sich öffnende Propter-Homines-Saal. Das rundum erneuerte und erweiterte Festspielhaus bietet nicht nur eine ideale Bühne für spektakuläre Operninszenierungen. Es ist seit seiner Vollendung auch ein Leuchtturm der Vorarlberger Baukunst.

Architecture as a stage

In a competition in 1992, Dietrich|Untertrifaller conceived the floor plan of the new Bregenz Festival House like a miniature city. They transformed the old theatre by Wilhelm Braun, which was inaugurated in 1980, in two stages using a collage of different building sections and newly constructed internal thoroughfare axes within a building with a sculptural appearance. To the south of the original building, they constructed a workshop stage and also added a connecting administration wing in a bar over the building sections to create a strong highlight. Since 2006, it has had a counterpart with a second continuous brace that penetrates the visitors' area on a lower level of the building and ends in the lakeside foyer. The public and internal accessing zones overlap at the lifts and thereby support the logistics of the Festival House. At times closed and cubic, and at others more animated, the building with its large window areas frames the lakeside stage, which has been expanded to a capacity of 6,800 and now also includes a theatre hall for an audience of 1,800, as well as a lakeside studio. They are joined by a restaurant, elegant foyers and the two-storey Propter Homines Hall that opens out onto the broad forecourt. The completely renovated and extended Festival House not only provides the ideal stage for spectacular opera productions. Since its completion, it has also been a beacon of Vorarlberg architecture.

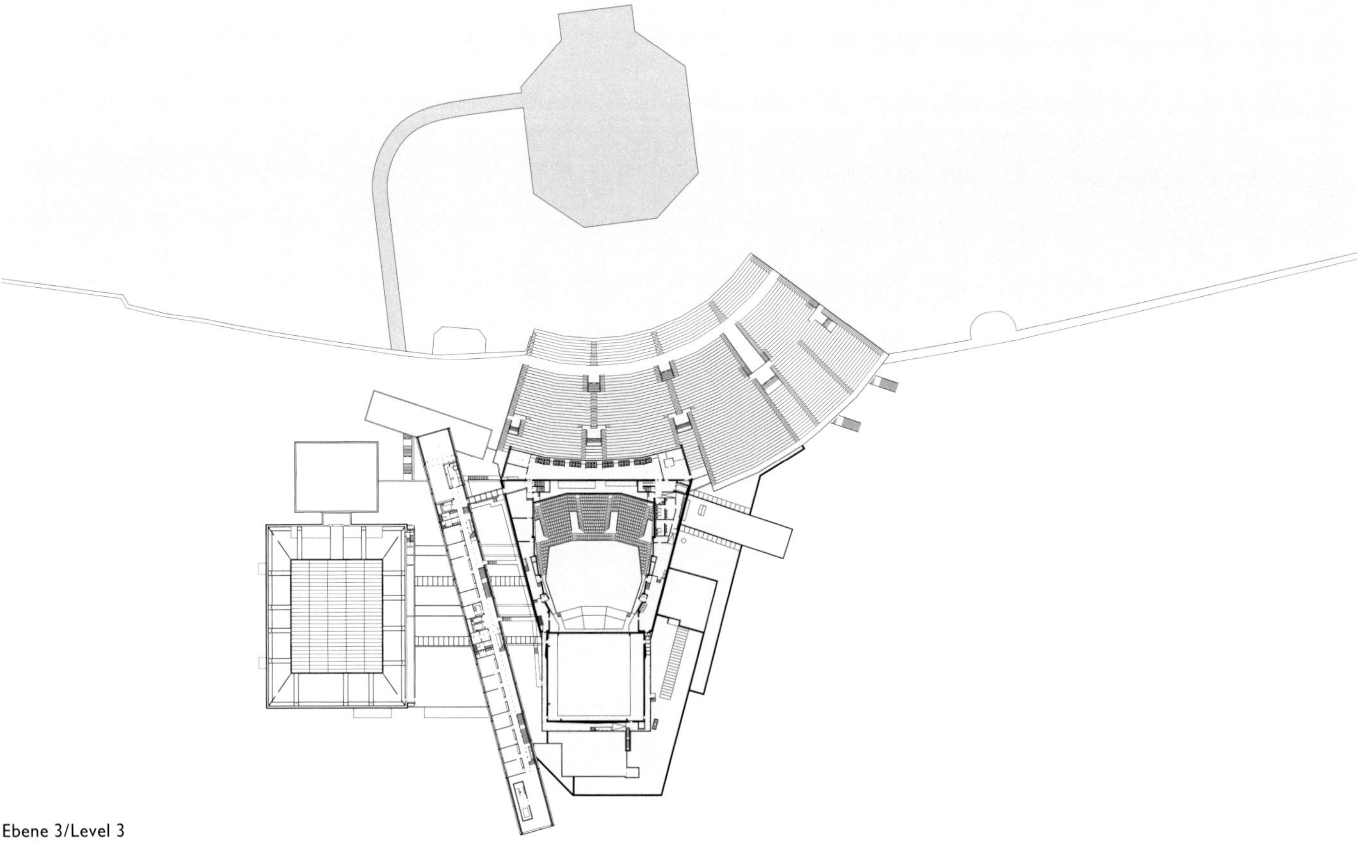

Ebene 3/Level 3

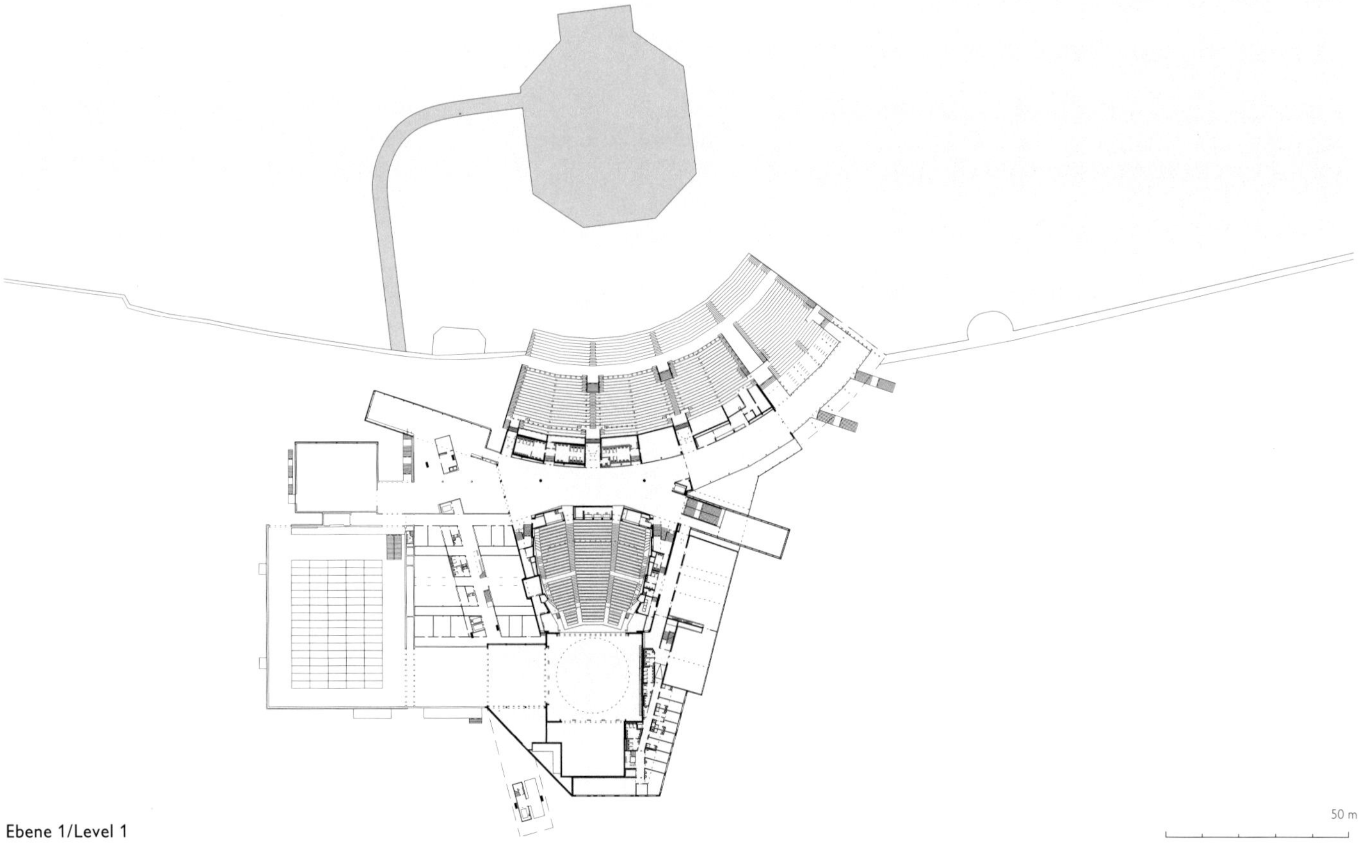

Ebene 1/Level 1

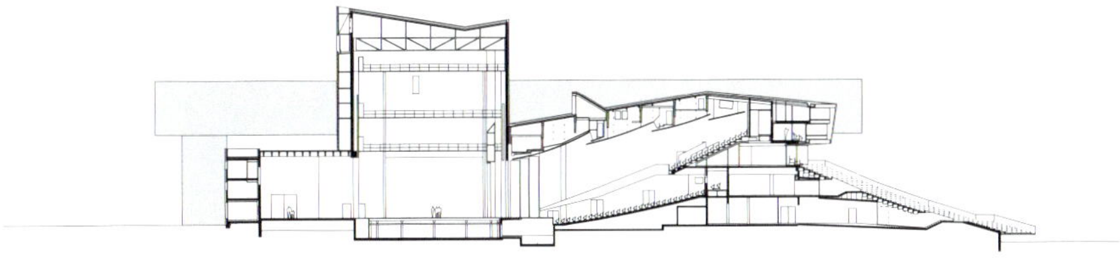

Schnitt/Cross-section

← propter h
→ bodensee
panorama
← tickets

Stadthalle F, Wien

Stadthalle F, Vienna

Wettbewerb/Competition: 2002
Ausführung/Construction: 2003–2006
Bauherr/Client: Stadthalle Wien
Planung/Planning: Dietrich|Untertrifaller
Projektleitung/Project management: P. Nussbaumer
Auszeichnung/Awards: 2006
Bauherrenpreis Österreich

Partner:
Projektmanagement/Project management, Haustechnik/Service engineers, Bauphysik/Building physics: Vasko Partner, Wien; Statik Beton/Statics concrete: Kollitsch Stanek, Wien; Statik Stahlbau/Statics steelwork: Zemler Raunicher, Wien; Elektro/Electrical engineer: Fleck, Wien; Bühnentechnik/Stage engineers: Kottke, Bayreuth; Akustik/Acoustics: Müller BBM, Planegg

Zwiegespräch mit einem Monument
Einer der bedeutendsten Nachkriegsbauten Wiens ist die 1958 von Roland Rainer realisierte Stadthalle. Sie galt es um die «Halle F», ein neues Gebäude für Konzerte, Kongresse und andere Veranstaltungen, zu erweitern. Den 2002 ausgeschriebenen Wettbewerb konnten Dietrich|Untertrifaller mit einem formal, funktional und städtebaulich gleichermassen überzeugenden Projekt für sich entscheiden. Sie platzierten das 2006 eröffnete, kristallin-vieleckige Gebäude passgenau in die Brache zwischen der Hütteldorfer Strasse und der Stadthalle, deren Streben sich wie Haifischzähne in der gläsernen Nordfassade des Neubaus spiegeln. Dank der präzisen Setzung optimiert dieser die zuvor für den Rainer-Bau wenig befriedigende urbanistische Situation. Um dem Volumen Schwere und Massigkeit zu nehmen, wurde es mittels einer stählernen Tragstruktur ins «Schweben» versetzt. Darunter weitet sich der von der Auskragung geschützte Vorplatz und die zu diesem hin verglaste Eingangshalle, von der aus man hinauf zum Theater gelangt. Der im Längsschnitt keilförmige Saal, der ganz in Rot gehalten ist, fasst rund 2000 Personen, denen zwei seitlich durch grosse Fensterflächen sich öffnende Pausenfoyers zur Verfügung stehen. Nachts werden sie zu faszinierenden Vitrinen und verwandeln die «Halle F» in ein gut sichtbares Aushängeschild des Wiener Kulturlebens.

Dialogue with a monument
One of the most important post-war buildings in Vienna is the Stadthalle, which was built in 1958 by Roland Rainer. The task was to extend it with a new building, "Halle F", for concerts, congresses and other events. The competition announced in 2002 was won by Dietrich|Untertrifaller with a formal, functional project that equally impressed in terms of its urban planning. They inserted the crystalline, polygonal building, which was opened in 2006, precisely into the layland between Hütteldorfer Strasse and the Stadthalle, thereby allowing its supports to reflect like shark teeth on the glazed northern façade of the new building. Thanks to that precise placement, the building optimises the rather unsatisfactory urban situation of the Rainer building. To remove the weightiness and scale of the volume, it was "floated" using a steel support structure. The forecourt spans out beneath the protective, overhanging building and the glazed entrance hall that reaches up to it, from where one can ascend into the theatre. The hall has a wedge-shaped longitudinal cross-section and can accommodate almost 2,000 people, who use the two adjoining interval foyers that have an open appearance due to their large window areas. At night, they become fascinating showcases and transform "Halle F" into a clearly visible flagship of Viennese cultural life.

halle F

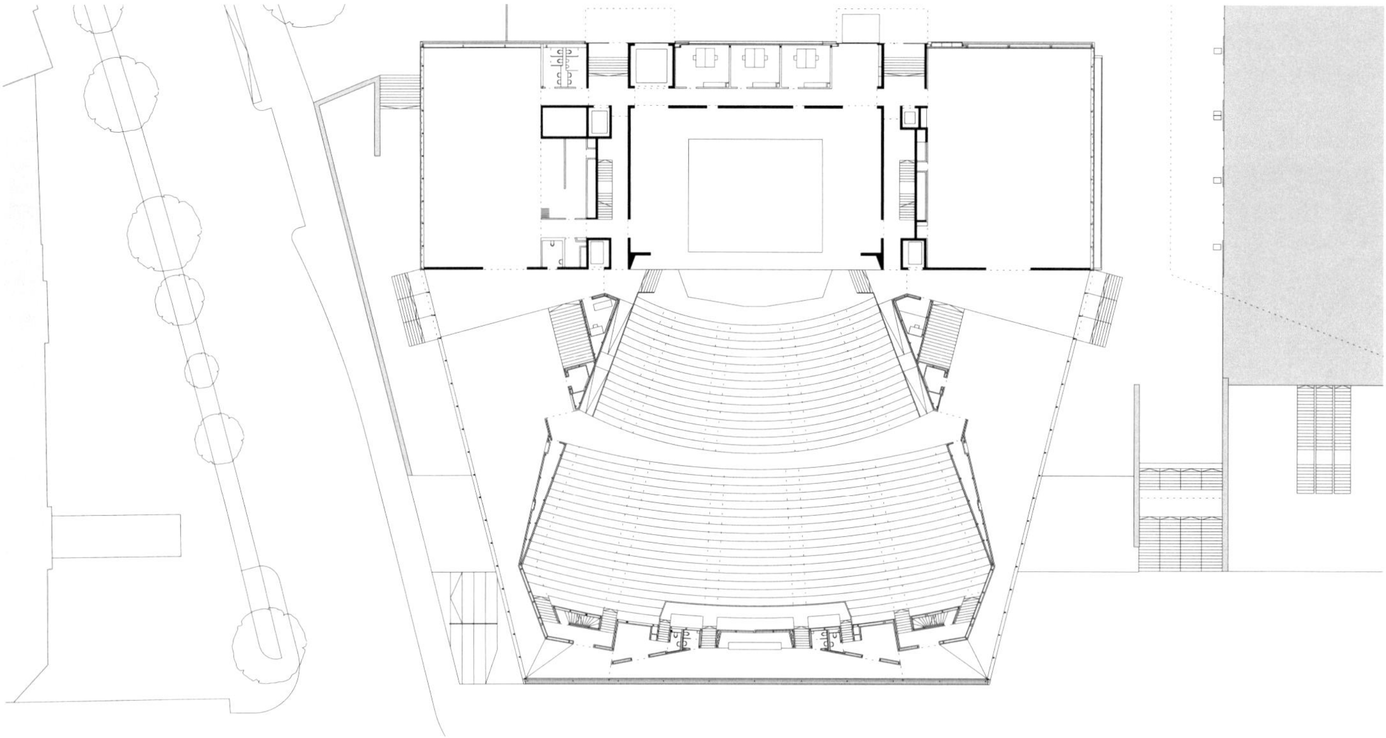

Ebene 1/Level 1

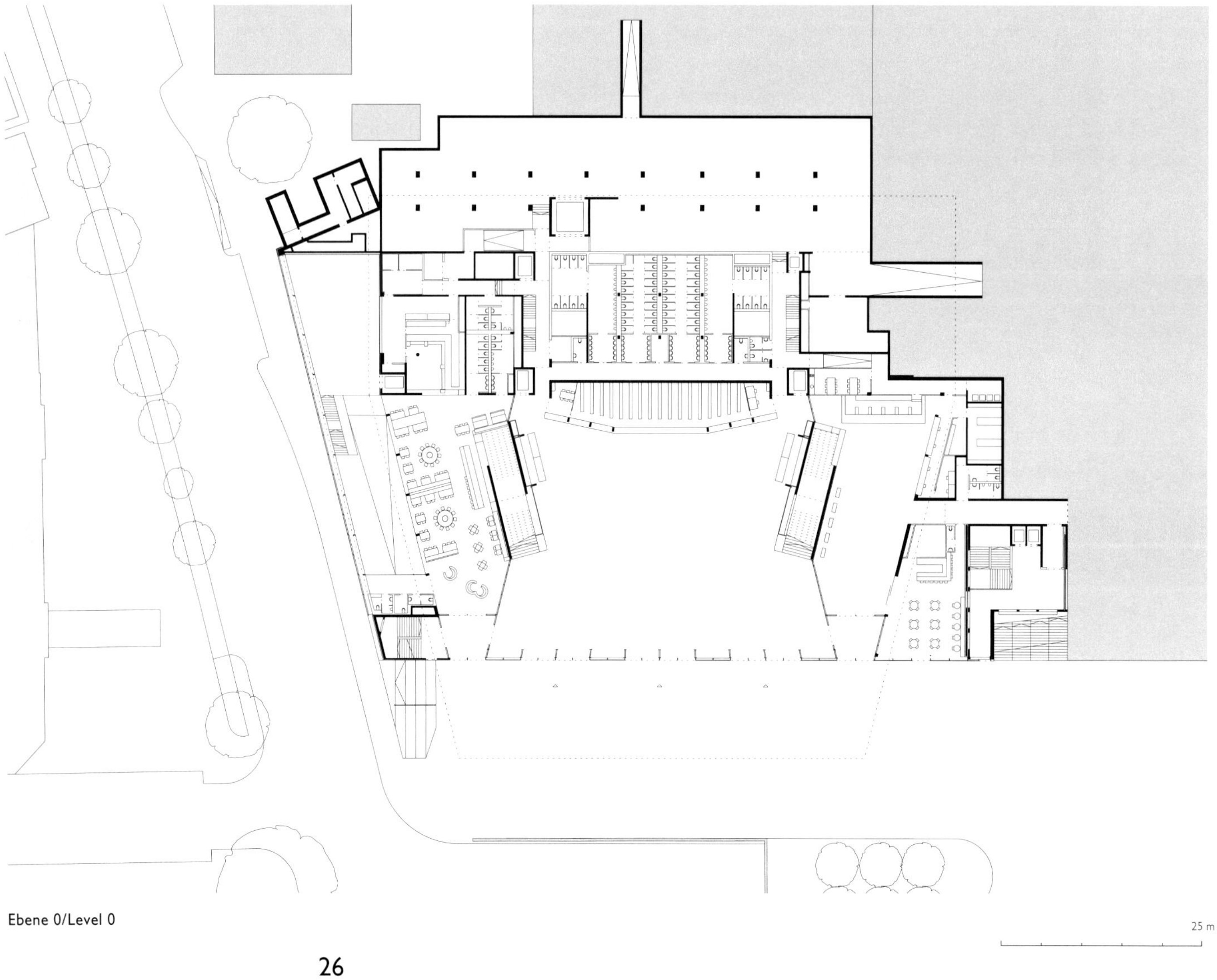

Ebene 0/Level 0

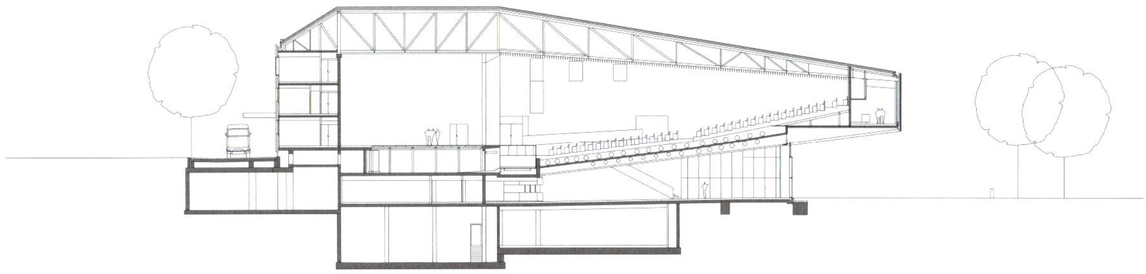

Schnitt/Cross-section

Angelika Kauffmann Museum, Schwarzenberg

Angelika Kauffmann Museum, Schwarzenberg

Ausführung/Construction: 2006–2007
Bauherr/Client: Gemeinde Schwarzenberg
Planung/Planning: Dietrich|Untertrifaller mit/with Baukultur
Projektleitung/Project management: H. Greber
Auszeichnung/Awards: 2010 *International Architectural Restauration Prize*; 2010 *Bauherrenpreis Vorarlberg*

Partner:
Bauleitung/Construction management: Baukultur, Schwarzenberg; Statik/Statics: Merz Kaufmann, Dornbirn; Haustechnik/Service engineers: Klimaplan, Hohenems; Elektro/Electrical engineer: Lingg, Schoppernau; Bauphysik/Building physics: Weithas, Hard; Akustik/Acoustics: Brüstle, Dornbirn

Baumeisterliche Präzision

Das Dorf Schwarzenberg im Bregenzerwald ist ein Juwel. Von hier stammt die in Chur geborene und in London und Rom berühmt gewordene Künstlerin Angelika Kauffmann (1741–1807), deren Werke heute unter anderem in Bregenz und Chur zu sehen sind. Da wollte Schwarzenberg nicht zurückstehen und der Malerin auch einen Ausstellungsraum widmen – und zwar in der Scheune des in einem ehemaligen Bauernhaus eingerichteten Heimatmuseums. Dietrich|Untertrifaller konzipierten 2006 eine die historische Hülle nur minimal tangierende Intervention. Der in die Scheune vorstossende, überdachte Eingangsbereich des Museums lässt sich durch ein wettergebräuntes Schiebetor so schliessen, dass von der modernen Konstruktion aus Holz und Glas nichts mehr zu sehen ist. Im Foyer treten die Einbauten aus hellem Weisstannenholz mit der dunklen Rückwand des Bauernhauses und den alten Dachbalken in einen spannungsvollen Dialog, während der Fussboden aus Fichte ein räumliches Kontinuum von der Eingangszone bis in den Ausstellungssaal erzeugt. Dieser wurde als flach gedecktes Haus im Haus in die Scheune eingefügt. Seine Längsseiten sind durch je drei Nischen gegliedert, zwischen denen verglaste Schlitze Blicke auf die alten Wände freigeben. Zu Recht wurde diese subtile baukünstlerische Transformation 2010 mit dem International Architectural Restauration Prize ausgezeichnet.

Architectural precision

The village Schwarzenberg in Bregenz Forest is a gem. It was the home of the artist Angelika Kauffmann (1741–1807), who was born in Chur and became famous in London and Rome. Today, her works are mainly displayed in Bregenz and Chur. To join the limelight, Schwarzenberg also dedicated an exhibition space to the artist – namely in the barn of a farmhouse that had formerly been used as a local historical museum. In 2006, Dietrich|Untertrifaller conceived an intervention that only minimally affected the historic shell. The barn's projecting, covered museum entrance area can be closed using a weathered sliding door to completely conceal the modern wood and glass structure. In the foyer, the installations consisting of silver fir timber enter into a tense dialogue with the dark rear wall of the farmhouse and the old roof beams, while the spruce flooring creates a spatial continuum from the entrance area to the exhibition hall. The flat-roof structure was inserted into the barn as a building within a building. Its longitudinal sides are structured by three niches, between which glazed slits reveal views of the old walls. The subtle architectural transformation was rightly awarded the 2010 International Architectural Restoration Prize.

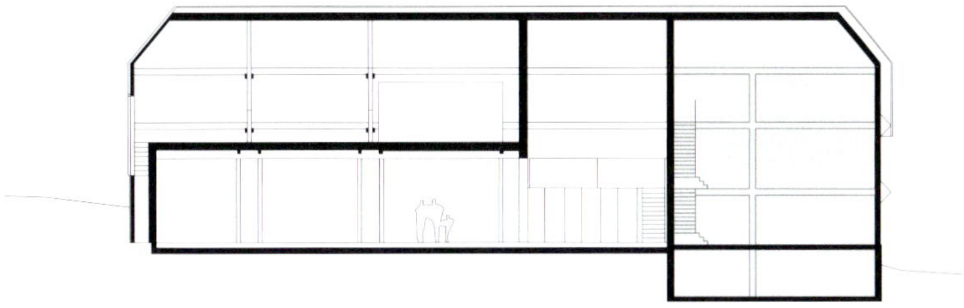

Längsschnitt/Longitudinal section

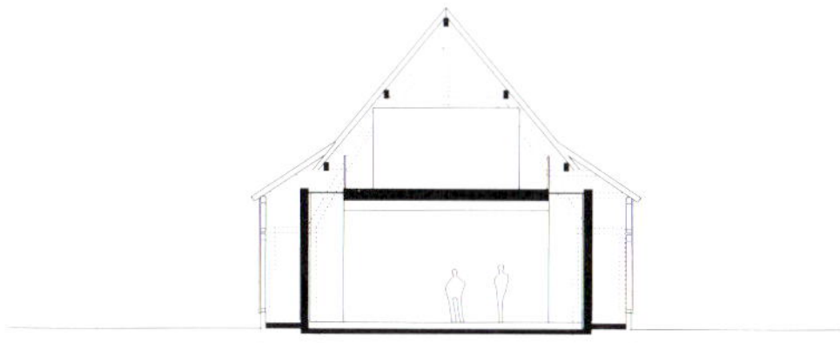

Schnitt/Cross-section

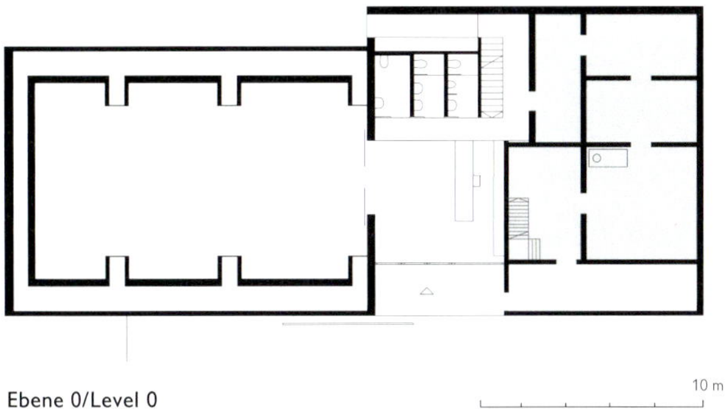

Ebene 0/Level 0

Fachhochschule Salzburg, Kuchl

Salzburg University of Applied Sciences, Kuchl

Wettbewerb/Competition: 2007
Ausführung/Construction: 2008–2009
Bauherr/Client: Weco FH Holztechnikum
Planung/Planning: Dietrich|Untertrifaller
Projektleitung/Project management: P. Nussbaumer, B. Breuer
Auszeichnungen/Awards: 2011 *Holzbaupreis*; 2011 *ZV-Bauherrenpreis*; 2010 *Architekturpreis Land Salzburg*

Partner:
Statik Holz/Statics wood: Pock, Spittal
Statik Beton/Statics concrete: Gaderer, Mondsee; Haustechnik/Service engineers: Burggraf, Salzburg; Bauphysik/Building physics: Graml, Wals; Elektro/Electrical engineer: Müller Uri, Enzersberg

Idealer Holzbau

Die heutigen Möglichkeiten der Holzbautechnik hinsichtlich Material, Design und Nachhaltigkeit sind das zentrale Thema des Erweiterungsbaus der Fachhochschule Salzburg in Kuchl. Der 2007 aus einem Wettbewerb hervorgegangene und zwei Jahre später vollendete Neubau, der sich L-förmig an das bestehende Haus anschliesst, gilt als erstes in Passivhausbauweise ganz aus Holz errichtetes Hochschulgebäude Österreichs. Den 400 Studierenden des Holztechnikums dient es als ein Best-Practice-Beispiel, von dem sie sich täglich neu anregen lassen können. Der von den mittigen Korridoren des alten Schulgebäudes aus über einen verglasten dreigeschossigen Verbindungsgang zugängliche Anbau bietet im Erdgeschoss neben dem Foyer und einem Seminarraum einen als Veranstaltungsraum nutzbaren Zeichensaal, im ersten Stock eine Bibliothek, ein Fotostudio, einen Projekt- sowie einen Seminarraum und im zweiten Stock drei weitere Seminarräume. Während die Stirnfronten des rahmenförmigen, durch eine Fluchttreppe aus Beton versteiften Holzbaus als tragende Wände ausgebildet sind, geben dreifach verglaste, teilweise durch fest installierte Weisstannen-Lamellen verschattete Fensterbänder den Blick auf die Berge frei. Mit dem Erweiterungsbau in Kuchl haben Dietrich|Untertrifaller einmal mehr bewiesen, dass ökologisches Bauen und zeitgemässe Formen sich gegenseitig nicht ausschliessen müssen.

Ideal wooden building

Today's potential for wooden construction with respect to materials, design and sustainability are the central theme of the extension building for the Salzburg University of Applied Sciences in Kuchl. Built two years after a competition in 2007, the new building connects with the existing complex in an L-shape and is regarded as the first university building in Austria to manage "passive house" construction standards despite being completely made of wood. It serves the 400 students in the Holztechnikum as a best practice example from which they can draw inspiration on a daily basis. The extension, which is accessed via the central corridors of the old university building and on through a glazed three-storey connecting walkway, accommodates a foyer and a seminar room on the ground floor, as well as an event room that can also be used as an art room. On the first floor, there are a library, a photo studio, a project room and a seminar room. Three more seminar rooms occupy the second floor. While the ends of the frame-shaped wooden building, which is reinforced by a concrete emergency stairway, are designed as load-bearing walls, triple glazed window bands that are partially shaded with fixed silver fir slats reveal the view towards the mountains. With the extension building in Kuchl, Dietrich|Untertrifaller have once again demonstrated how ecological construction and contemporary forms are not mutually incompatible.

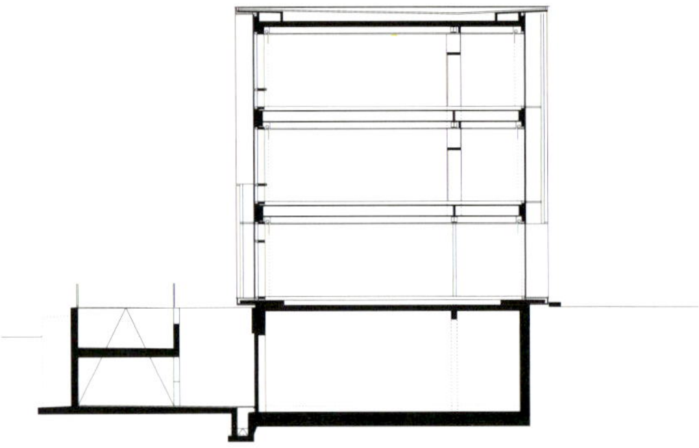

Schnitt/Cross-section

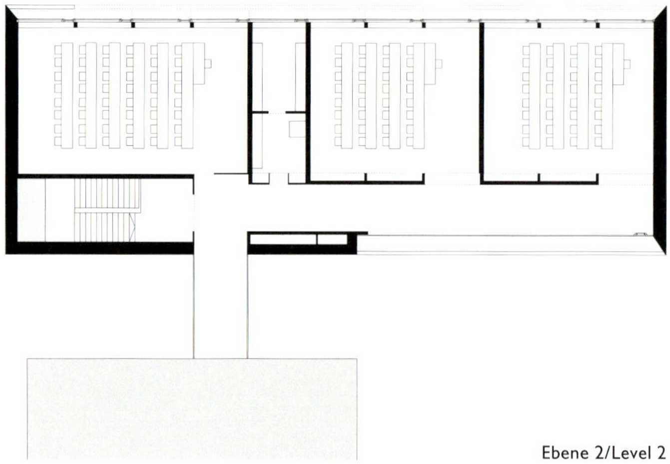

Ebene 2/Level 2

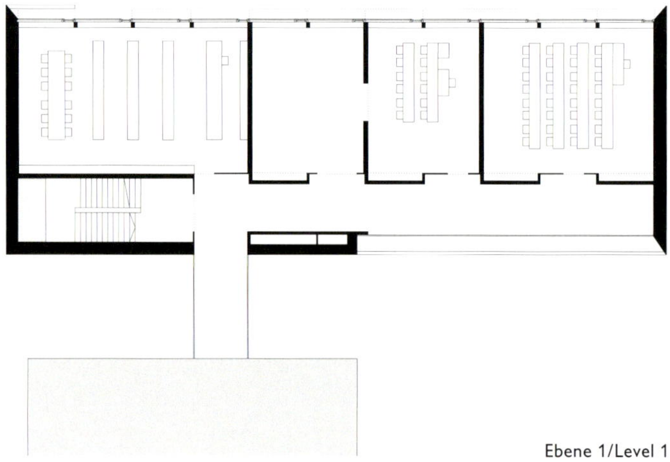

Ebene 1/Level 1

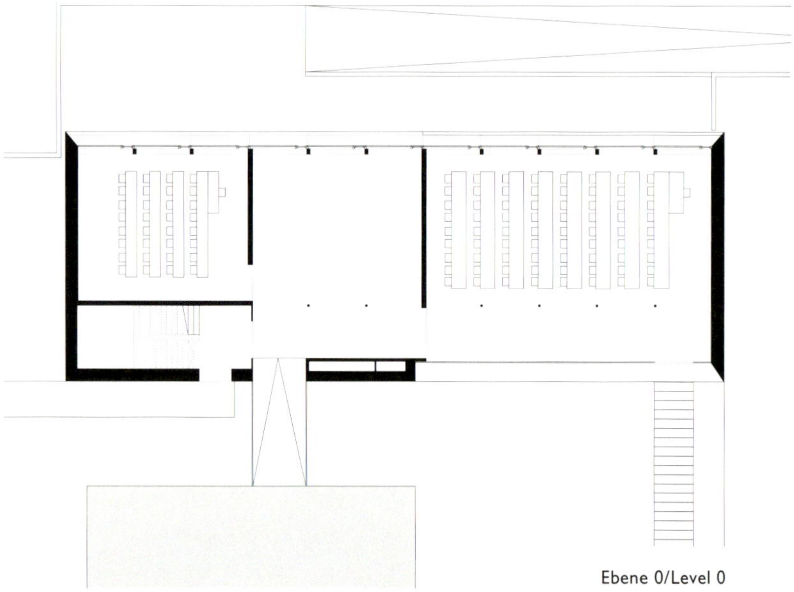

Ebene 0/Level 0

ETH Sport Center, Zürich

ETH Sports Centre, Zurich

Ausführung/Construction: 2006–2009
Wettbewerb/Competition: 2004
Bauherr/Client: ETH Zürich
Planung/Planning: Dietrich|Untertrifaller mit/with Ch. Stäheli
Projektleitung/Project management: P. Nussbaumer
Auszeichnungen/Awards: 2011 *Sustainable Architecture*; 2011 *Österreichischer Baupreis*; 2011 *IOC-IAKS Award*; 2012 *AIT-Award*

Partner:
Statik/Statics: Mader Flatz Rissi, Bregenz und/and SHP, Zürich; Haustechnik/Service engineers: GMI, Dornbirn; Licht/Light: Hecht, Rankweil; Akustik/Acoustics: Brüstle, Dornbirn; Bauphysik/Building physics: Weithas, Hard; Geologe/Geologist: Andres, St. Gallen; Fassadenplanung/Façade planning: Mosbacher, Schwarzach; Kostenplanung/Financial planning: Baudata, Schaan; Signaletik/Guidance system: TGG St. Gallen

Bauen auf dem Campus

Der Höhenzug über dem einstigen Weinbauerndorf Höngg ist ein von den Zürchern gern genutzter Naherholungsraum. Hier befindet sich aber auch der schnell wachsende Hönggerberg-Campus Science City auf dem Hönggerberg der Eidgenössischen Technischen Hochschule (ETH) Zürich. Am Ostrand der von Feldern und Wäldern umgebenen Anlage sollte ein Sportzentrum entstehen. Den prestigeträchtigen Bauauftrag konnten sich Dietrich|Untertrifaller gemeinsam mit Christof Stäheli 2004 mit einem architektonisch und urbanistisch gleichermassen einleuchtenden Wettbewerbsprojekt sichern. Das 2009 vollendete Bauwerk ist ganz aus der Hangtopografie hergeleitet und besteht aus einem System von Rechtecken, Dreiecken und Parallelogrammen. Dem Campus wendet es seine städtische Eingangsfassade zu, bestehend aus kristallin geknickten, grünen Glasscheiben. Dahinter aber verschwindet das nach neuesten ökologischen Erkenntnissen errichtete Sport Center in der leicht ansteigenden Landschaft. Selbst das Dach ist begrünt und kann für Freiluftsport genutzt werden. Im Innern zieht neben dem elegant möblierten Foyer eine abgesenkte Dreifachturnhalle mit Zuschauerrängen die Aufmerksamkeit auf sich. Der trendige Kraftraum sowie die Tanz- und Gymnastiksäle bleiben hingegen für Besucher unsichtbar. Dafür können sie ins Grüne blicken und dabei erkennen, wie einfühlsam sich beim Sport Center Natur und Architektur verschränken.

Building on campus

The mountain range above the former wine-growing village of Höngg is popular among Zurich residents as a local recreation area. It is also the location of the rapidly growing Hönggerberg-Campus Science City on the Hönggerberg, part of the Swiss Federal Institute of Technology Zurich (ETH). A sports centre was planned at the eastern periphery of the estate, which is surrounded by fields and forests. In 2004, the prestigious building contract was awarded to Dietrich|Untertrifaller together with Christof Stäheli, who presented an architecturally and urbanistically impressive competition project. The building was completed in 2009, is entirely derived from the topography of the slope and consists of a system of quadrangles, triangles and parallelograms. Its urban entrance façade faces the campus and is made of crystalline, angled green glass panes. Behind it however, the sports centre, which was built according to the latest ecological standards, blends into the gently rising landscape. Even the roof is green and can be used for open-air sports. Inside, the elegantly furnished foyer and the sunken triple sports hall with spectator stands draw attention to themselves. By contrast, the trendy weight-training room, the dance hall and gymnastics hall remain invisible to visitors. They can however enjoy the view of the green landscape and recognise how sensitively the Sports Centre manages to combine nature and architecture.

33
Sport Center

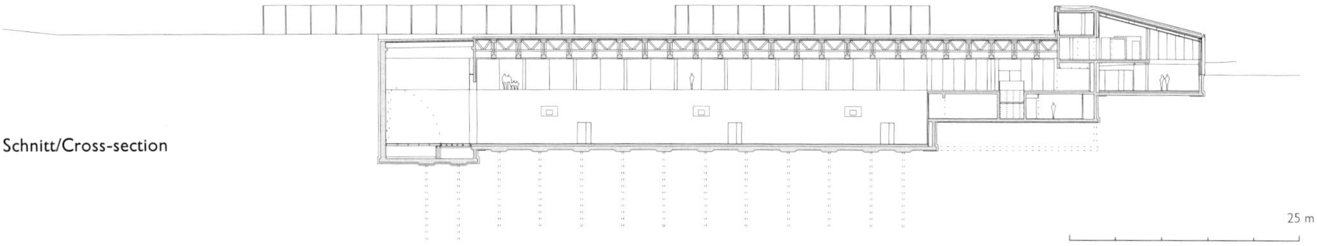

Schnitt/Cross-section

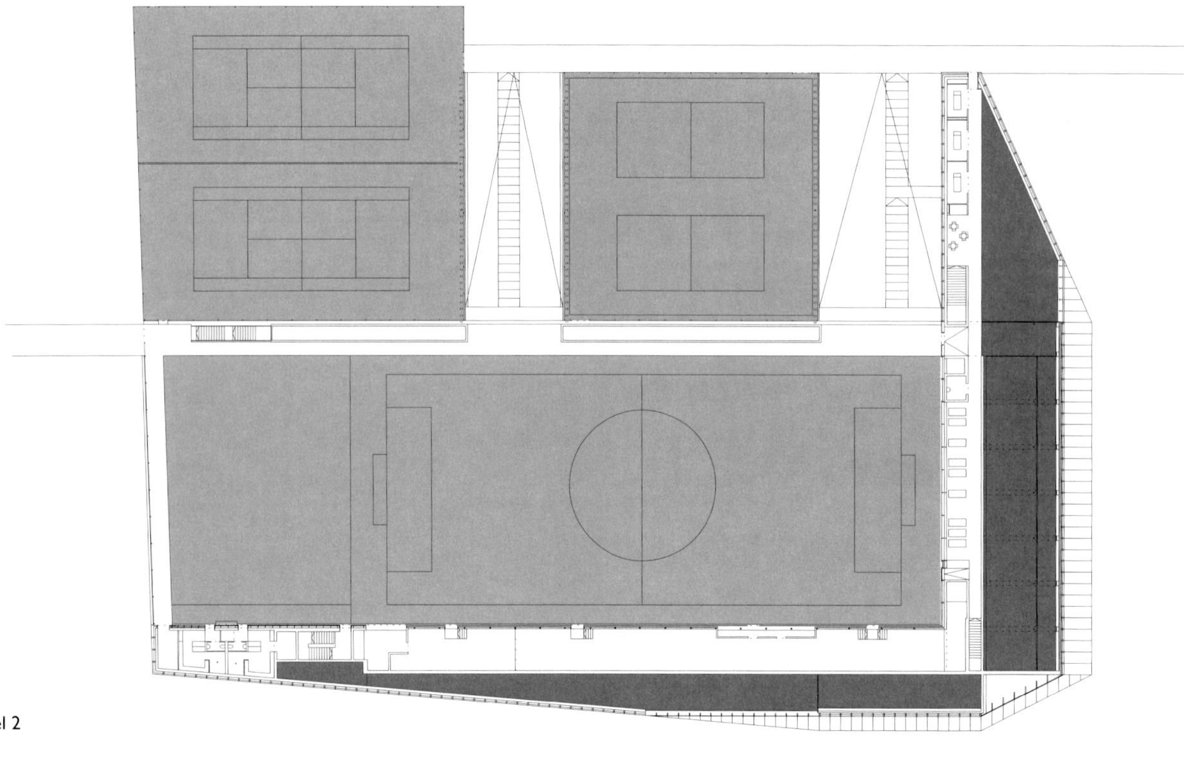

Ebene 2/Level 2

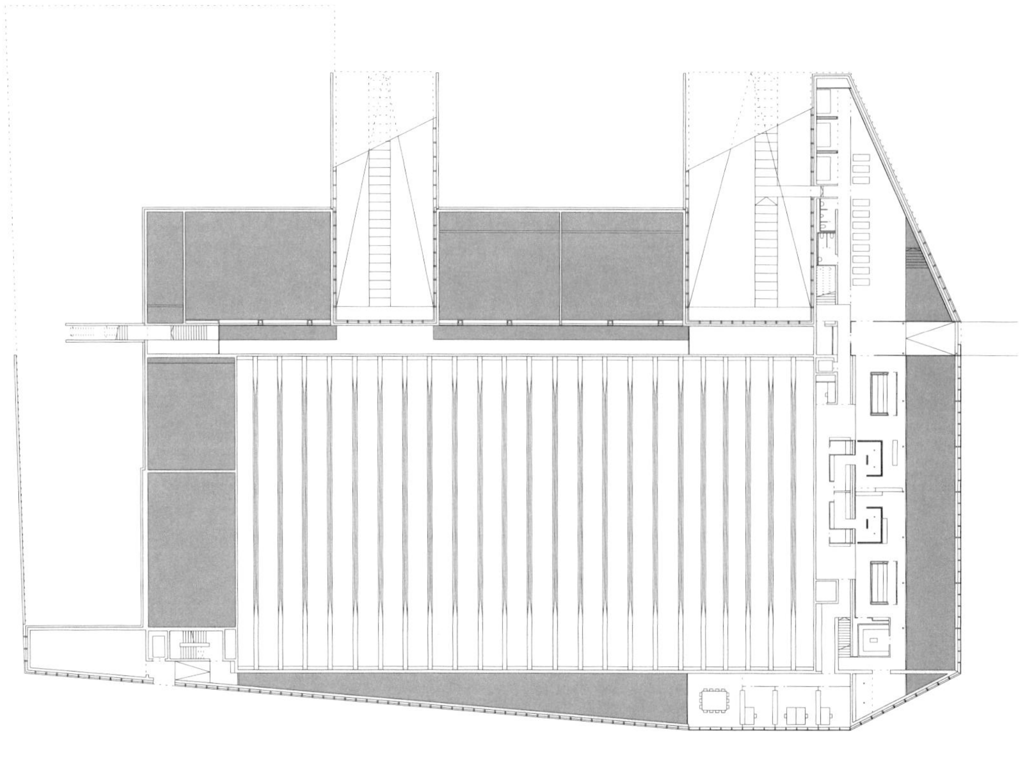

Ebene 1/Level 1

Sport Center
33

Sport Wellness
Verpflegung
Information

Arena 1

Reka Feriendorf, Urnäsch

Reka Holiday Village, Urnäsch

Ausführung/Construction: 2006–2007
Bauherr/Client: Feriendorf Urnäsch
Planung/Planning: Dietrich|Untertrifaller mit/with R. Gnaiger
Projektleitung/Project management: G. Prechter, N. Haumer
Auszeichnungen/Awards: 2008 *Minergie-Eco*; 2008 *Europäischer Dorferneuerungspreis*; 2009 *Holzpreis Schweiz Lignum*; 2011 *Gutes Bauen Ostschweiz*

Partner:
Bauleitung/Construction management: Amann Partner, Stein; Haustechnik/Service engineers: Euplan, Herisau; Statik Holz/Statics wood: SJB Kempter Fitze, Herisau; Statik Beton/Statics concrete: Moggi, Herisau; Bauphysik/Building physics: Weithas, Hard; Elektro/Electrical engineer: Graf, Herisau; Landschaftsarchitektur/Landscape architecture: Engeler, Herisau

Siedlung am Dorfrand
Bauen in einer intakten Umgebung verlangt viel Fingerspitzengefühl. Als es im Jahr 2000 darum ging, in der Appenzeller Gemeinde Urnäsch den Bau einer Feriensiedlung am Übergang vom malerischen Dorfkern zur locker mit Höfen besetzten Hügellandschaft zu planen, schlugen Dietrich|Untertrifaller zusammen mit Roland Gnaiger ein kleines, teppichartig dichtes Geflecht von Flachdachbauten vor. Die mit dem Minergie-Eco-Label ausgezeichnete Anlage, die sich formal deutlich von den historischen Häusern unterscheidet, aber mit ihren Holzfassaden und Bandfenstern traditionelle Elemente neu interpretiert, konnte 2007 eröffnet werden. Der Hauptstrasse entlang zieht sich ein aus vier abgetreppten Gemeinschaftsbauten bestehender Riegel, in welchem unter anderem die Rezeption, der Veranstaltungssaal, die Bibliothek, das Hallenbad, der Jugendraum und der Kleintierstall untergebracht sind. Dahinter bilden drei abgewinkelte Wohntrakte unterschiedlich grosse Höfe, zu denen sich die 50 über ein bis fünf Zimmer verfügenden Ferienwohnungen im Erd- und im Obergeschoss mit Loggien öffnen. Die Flachdächer, die aufgrund der bergigen Topografie von oben als fünfte Fassade wahrgenommen werden, sind begrünt und fügen sich diskret in die dörfliche Szenerie ein. Entstanden ist eine gebaute Landschaft, die den Architekten zufolge «eher Teil der Topografie als Teil des Dorfes ist.»

Estate on the village outskirts
Building in an intact environment requires a great deal of sensitivity. In 2000, the task was to plan a holiday settlement in the Appenzell community of Urnäsch, above the picturesque village centre on a hillside landscape loosely populated with farms. Dietrich|Untertrifaller, together with Roland Gnaiger, proposed a small, carpet-like texture of flat-roofed buildings. The estate has been awarded the Minergie Eco-Label and has strongly contrasting forms from the historic buildings, but does reinterpret traditional elements through the wooden façades and window bands. It was opened in 2007. Aligned along the main street, a bar of four staggered common buildings accommodates a reception, the event hall, the library, the indoor swimming pool, the youth centre, stables for small animals and other rooms. Behind it, three angled residential wings create courtyards with different sizes, towards which the 50 holiday apartments on the ground floor and upper level face, each with one to five rooms and a loggia. The flat roofs, which are perceived from above as a fifth façade due to the mountainous topography, are green and discreetly integrated into the village scenery. The result is a well-built landscape which the architects regard to be, “more a part of the topography than part of the village.”

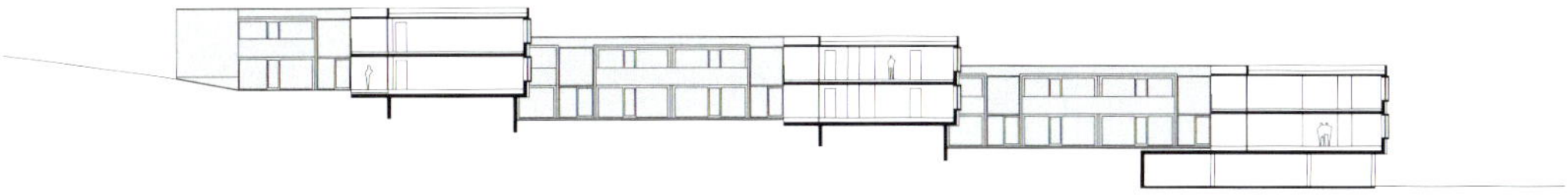

Schnitt/Cross-section

Ebene 0/Level 0

Haus LK, Hard

House LK, Hard

Ausführung/Construction: 2008–2009
Bauherr/Client: Familie LK
Planung/Planning: Dietrich|Untertrifaller
Projektleitung/Project management: S. Gaudl

Partner:
Statik/Statics: Mader Flatz, Bregenz
Haustechnik/Service engineers: GMI Ingenieure, Dornbirn;
Elektro/Electrical engineer: Hecht, Rankweil; Bauleitung/Construction management: Künz, Hard

Gestapelte Betonbalken

Einfamilienhäuser dienen Dietrich|Untertrifaller oft als Objekte der baukünstlerischen Recherche. Neben einfachen, präzise in die Dörfer und Landschaften Vorarlbergs eingepassten Holzhäusern realisieren sie auch elegante Villen – meist in aussichtsreichen Hanglagen. Eine Ausnahme bildet die 2009 in der Rheinebene bei Hard am Bodensee vollendete Villa LK. Um Sicht und Raum zu schaffen, wurde das kalifornisch mondän anmutende Haus in der Nordostecke einer grossen, von alten Eschen und Weiden flankierten Wiese errichtet. Am balkenartig in West-Ost-Richtung sich erstreckenden Erdgeschoss entlang gelangt man zum wettergeschützten Eingangsbereich. Dieser befindet sich unter der Auskragung des Obergeschosses, das als zweiter Balken fast wie eine Wippe den unteren Bauteil rechtwinklig überlagert. Auch gartenseitig greift dieser Balken weit aus und überdacht die vorgelagerte Küche und den Sitzplatz im Freien. Im Innern fungiert die Treppenhalle als Drehscheibe des Hauses. Nach rechts gelangt man in den Salon, ins Büro, das auf ein begrüntes Atrium blickt, sowie zur Einliegerwohnung. Geradeaus geht es in die dreiseitig verglaste Wohnküche, während man treppauf die Schlafzimmer mit Terrassen und Seesicht erreicht. Überall aber betonen klare Formen, Sichtbeton und Glas die abstrakte Plastizität dieser Villenarchitektur.

Stacked concrete bars

Dietrich|Untertrifaller often use single-family homes as objects of architectural research. In addition to simple wooden houses that are precisely inserted into the Vorarlberg villages and landscapes, they also build elegant villas – mostly on slopes with fine views. One exception is the Villa LK, which was built in the Rhine valley near Hard by Lake Constance. To create a view and space, a large meadow flanked by old ash and willow trees was created at the north-eastern corner of the house, which has a sophisticated, Californian style. The sheltered entrance area is reached along the bar-like ground floor that is aligned in a west-east direction. It is situated beneath the protruding upper floor, a second perpendicular bar that overlaps the lower section almost like a seesaw. On the garden side, that bar reaches far out and covers the kitchen in front and the outside seating area. Inside, the staircase acts as the building's hub. Turning right, one enters the salon, the office with its view of the green atrium, and the guest apartment. Straight ahead, there is the combined kitchen and living room, while going up the stairs, one reaches the bedrooms with terraces and their view of the lake. Everywhere, clear forms, fair-faced concrete and glass highlight the abstract, sculptural nature of this villa architecture.

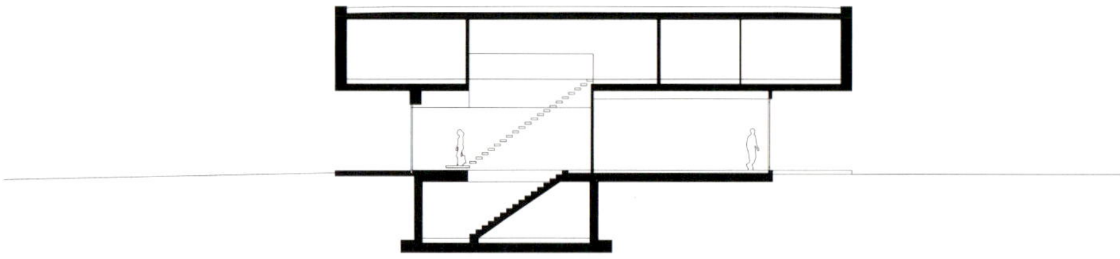

Schnitt/Cross-section

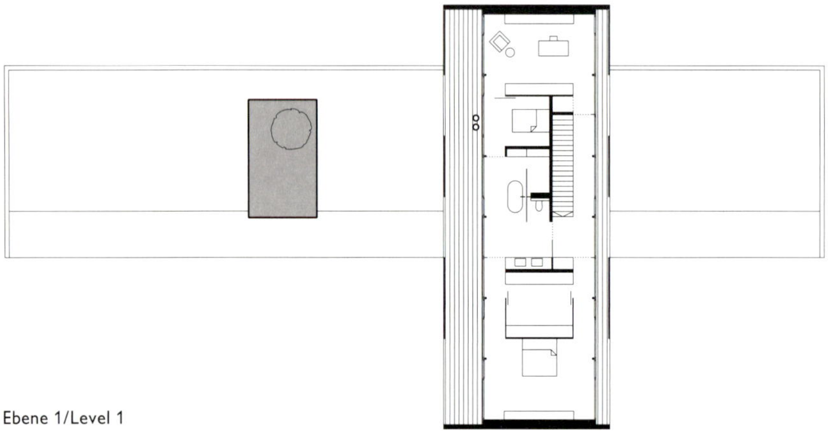

Ebene 1/Level 1

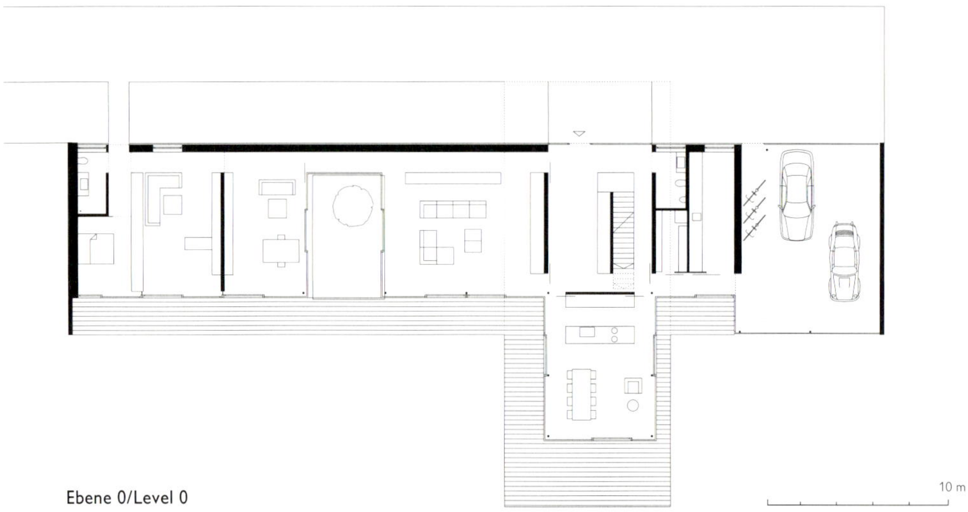

Ebene 0/Level 0

Haus A, Dornbirn

House A, Dornbirn

Ausführung/Construction: 2008–2009
Bauherr/Client: Familie A
Planung/Planning: Dietrich|Untertrifaller
Projektleitung/Project management: P. Nussbaumer, F. Kruck
Auszeichnungen/Awards: 2011 *Häuser Award*; 2011 *Holzbaupreis Vorarlberg*

Partner:
Statik/Statics: Mader Flatz, Bregenz
Haustechnik/Services engineer: GMI, Dornbirn: Elektro/Electrical engineer: Hecht, Rankweil

Villa am Waldrand

Locker über Hügel und Hänge verstreute Einzelhöfe sind typisch für Vorarlberg. Dieser alemannischen Siedlungsweise entsprechend, steht das 2009 von Dietrich|Untertrifaller in Kehlegg bei Dornbirn errichtete Haus A oben an einem nach Süden abfallenden Wiesenhang. Der mit handwerklichem Können in neuester Holzbautechnik ausgeführte Bau überzeugt durch schöne Proportionen und logische Grundrisse – genau wie die früher schon von Dietrich|Untertrifaller im Bregenzerwald realisierten Einfamilienhäuser. Das sorgsam in die Böschung eingefügte Gebäude ist talseitig zwei- und strassenseitig eingeschossig. Dort weitet sich ein kleiner, vom Haus, dem Nebengebäude und einer Einfriedung definierter Vorplatz, wie man ihn ähnlich auch bei Bauernhöfen finden kann. Im Innern des Hauses, das mit seinem Giebeldach und den an den Bregenzerwälder «Schopf» erinnernden Loggien zeitlos anmutet, wechselt sich die moderne Holzausstattung mit raumhohen Fensterfronten ab. Vom offenen Wohn- und Essbereich, an den nach Westen eine kleine Einliegerwohnung anschliesst, führt eine Treppe hinunter zu den bergseitig durch einen Flur erschlossenen Schlafzimmern. Zur Aussicht hin ist ihnen ein überdeckter Sitzplatz im Freien vorgelagert, wo man den urbanen Wohnkomfort im Einklang mit der Natur des Firstgebietes geniessen kann.

Villa on the edge of a forest

Individual farms loosely scattered over the hills and slopes are typical for the Vorarlberg region. In accordance with that Alemannic form of settlement, Haus A, which was built by Dietrich|Untertrifaller in 2009 in Kehlegg near Dornbirn, is situated upon a meadow that slopes down towards the south. The building was constructed with skilled craftsmanship using state of the art wooden building techniques and impresses with its fine proportions and logical floor plans – just like the earlier single family homes built by Dietrich|Untertrifaller in Bregenz Forest. The building is carefully inserted into the slope and has two floors on the slope side and one towards the street. In front of it, a small forecourt defined by the house, the auxiliary building and an enclosure recalls similar spaces on farms. Inside the house, which has a timeless appearance due to the gabled roof and loggias that are reminiscent of Bregenz Forest "Schopf" verandas, modern wooden fittings alternate with room-high window fronts. From the open living and dining area, which adjoins with a small guest apartment to the west, a staircase leads downwards along a hall to the bedrooms on the slope side. Towards the view, there is a covered outside seating area where one can enjoy the comfort of an urban home in harmony with the nature of the First region.

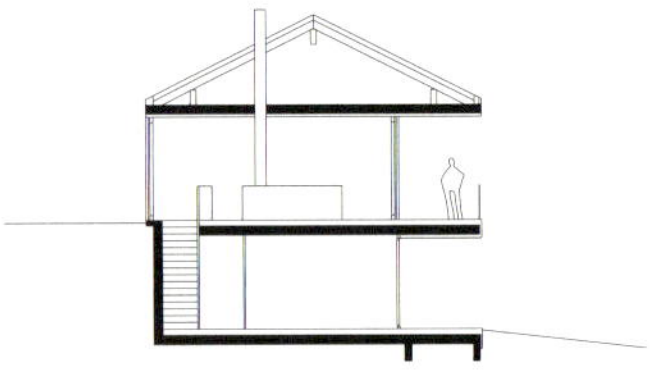

Schnitt/Cross-section

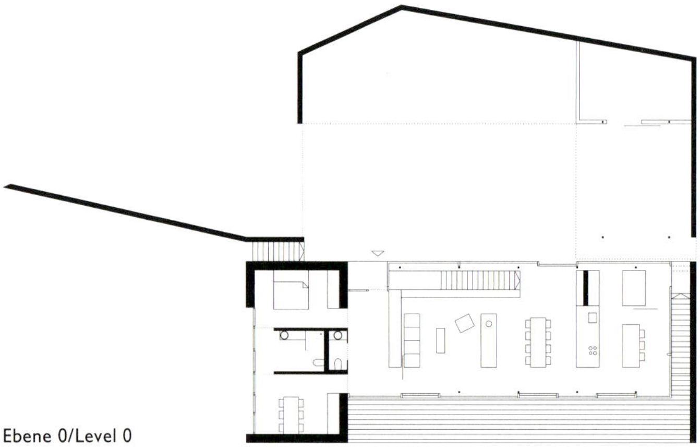

Ebene 0/Level 0

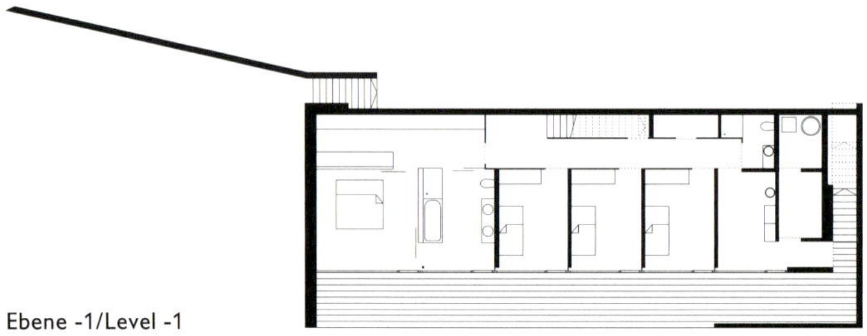

Ebene -1/Level -1

10 m

Werkverzeichnis/List of Works

Auswahl Bauten und Projekte/Selection of Buildings and Projects

1996		Ausbau Altmannfabrik, Bregenz A (Abb. S. 6)
		Café-Bar W. Greil, Innsbruck A
	1	Wohnsiedlung Spinnereistrasse, Hard A
		Haus B, Bregenz A (Abb. S. 9)
		Wohnanlage Schillerstrasse, Bregenz A
1997		Erweiterung Festspielhaus, Bregenz A (Bauabschnitt 1)
1998		Verwaltungsgebäude Rupp Cheese Innovation, Lochau A (Abb. S. 8)
		Haus S, Egg A (Abb. S. 12)
		Ortszentrum, Wolfurt A
1999		Revitalisierung Fachhochschule, Dornbirn A (mit Ch. Lenz)
	2	Haus R, Schnepfau A (Abb. S. 12)
		Kindergarten Rosenlächerstrasse, Lustenau A (Abb. S. 9)
2000		Firmengebäude Walch's Event Catering, Lustenau A (Abb. S. 8)
		Haus L, Bregenz A
		Umbau Konzernzentrale Hilti, Schaan FL
2001	**3**	arlberg.well.com, St. Anton A (Abb. S. 10)
	4	Café Deli Naschmarkt, Wien A
2002	**5**	Umbau Foyer und Restaurant Schauspielhaus, Wien A
		Haus R, Bregenz A (Abb. S. 12)
2003	**6**	Haus B, Klaus A
		Umbau und Erweiterung Gymnasium Schoren, Dornbirn A

1

2

3

4

5

6

2003	**7**	Museum Inatura, Dornbirn A (mit Ch. Lenz, H. Kaufmann)
		Hauptschule Klaus Weiler Fraxern, Klaus A (Abb. S. 10)
	8	Kaffeehaus Deuringstrasse elf, Bregenz A
	9	Haus K, Schwarzenberg A (Abb. S. 12)
2004	**10**	Areal der Vorarlberger Kraftwerke, Bregenz A
	11	Bürgerhaus, Bregenz A
	12	Kindergarten und Musikprobelokal, Egg A
2005		Wohn- und Geschäftshaus *Am Hafen*, Bregenz A (Abb. S. 14)
	13	Feuerwehr- und Bergrettungshaus, Mellau A
		Haus S, Lech A
	14	Ferienhaus A, Davos CH
2006		Wohn- und Geschäftshaus *Office am See*, Bregenz A (Abb. S. 14)
		Wiener Stadthalle F, Wien A
		Eurospar Vorkloster, Bregenz A (Abb. S. 11)
		Umbau und Erweiterung Festspielhaus (Bauabschnitt 2), Bregenz A
	15	Ausbau Flachgasse 35–37, Wien A
	16	Wohnanlage Mühlweg, Wien A (Abb. S. 13)
2007		Museum Angelika Kauffmann, Schwarzenberg A (mit Baukultur)
		Revitalisierung Velag Areal, Bregenz A

7

8

9

10

11

12

2008		Feriendorf Reka, Urnäsch CH (mit R. Gnaiger)
	17	Sanierung Hypobank-Zentrale, Bregenz A (Abb. S. 15)
2009		Fachhochschulgebäude Salzburg, Kuchl A (Abb. S. 13)
		ETH Sport Center, Zürich CH (mit Ch. Stäheli)
	18	Ulmer-Areal, Dornbirn A
		Haus LK, Hard A (Abb. S. 13)
		Gartensiedlung Lobaugasse, Wien A
		Haus A, Dornbirn A (Abb. S. 11)
	19	Sanierung Hotel Rote Wand, Lech A
	20	Geschäftshaus Marktstrasse 33, Dornbirn A
2011		Areal am Garnmarkt, Götzis A
	21	Feuerwehr Thal, Sulzberg A
	22	Haus SF, Dornbirn A
		Sportgelände, Hittisau A
	23	Sanierung Volksschule Wallenmahd, Dornbirn A
		Überbauung *Lineaar*, Aarau CH (mit Ch. Stäheli; Abb. S. 11)

13

14

15

16

17

18

2012 **24** Wohnanlage Widum, Wetzikon CH (mit Ch. Stäheli)
Grundschule, Kalbach D (mit M. Schmitt; Abb. S. 17)
Unternehmenszentrale I+R Gruppe, Lauterach A
Diem-Werke, Hörbranz A

Laufende Projekte/Current projects
2013 Europazentrum Gut Hochreute, Immenstadt D (mit R. Gnaiger)
Duo Dreilindenhang, St. Gallen CH (mit Ch. Stäheli)
Wohnanlage Dorfstrasse, Feldkirch A
2014 Hochschule für Kunst, Nancy F (mit Ch. Zoméno; Abb. S. 16)
Medizinisches Zentrum, Appenzell CH (mit Ch. Stäheli)
Omicron Campus, Klaus A
2015 Schule Jean Monnet, Broons F (mit Colas-Durand; Abb. S. 17)
Sportzentrum, Longvic F (mit Sénéchal-Auclair; Abb. S. 17)
2016 Neubaugürtel Kokerei Zollverein, Essen D (Abb. S. 17)
Konzerthaus, Strassburg F (mit Rey-Lucquet; Abb. S. 16)
2017 Seequartier beim Bahnhof, Bregenz A (Abb. S. 16)

19

20

21

22

23

24

Helmut Dietrich

1957	geboren in Mellau, Vorarlberg A
1977–1985	Architekturstudium an der Techn. Universität Wien A – Diplom bei Ernst Hiesmayr
1983–1986	Mitarbeit im Studio Paolo Piva, Biella und Venedig I
1986–1993	Bürogemeinschaft mit Christian Lenz, Hermann Kaufmann und Elmar Gmeiner, Schwarzach A; Arbeitsgemeinschaft mit Much Untertrifaller jun. und sen., Bregenz A
1994	Gründung Dietrich|Untertrifaller Architekten, Bregenz A; 2004 Büro Wien A; 2005 Büro St. Gallen CH

Gastprofessuren und Lehraufträge an verschiedenen Universitäten (Wien A, Vaduz FL, Linz A, Udine I, Nancy F)
Mitglied verschiedener Fachgremien (Vorarlberger Architekturinstitut, Wettbewerbsausschuss Vorarlberg, Gestaltungsbeirat in Steyr A, Bludenz A, Widnau CH, Lustenau A und Mellau A)

1957	Born in Mellau, Vorarlberg, A
1977–1985	Studied Architecture at the Vienna University of Technology – graduated under Ernst Hiesmayr
1983–1986	Employed by Studio Paolo Piva, Biella and Venice, I
1986–1993	Joint office with Christian Lenz, Hermann Kaufmann and Elmar Gmeiner, Schwarzach, A; Partnership with Much Untertrifaller Jr. and Sr., Bregenz A
1994	Founded Dietrich|Untertrifaller Architekten, Bregenz A; 2004 Vienna A office; 2005 St. Gallen CH office

Guest Professor at various universities (Vienna A, Vaduz FL, Linz A, Udine I, Nancy F)
Member of various expert committees (Vorarlberg Institute of Architecture, Vorarlberg Competition Commitee, Architecture Advisory Committee in Steyr A, Bludenz A, Widnau CH, Lustenau A and Mellau A)

Much Untertrifaller

1959	geboren in Bregenz, Vorarlberg A
1979–1988	Architekturstudium an der Techn. Universität Wien A – Diplom bei Ernst Hiesmayr
1982–1985	Mitarbeit im Architekturbüro Much Untertrifaller sen., Bregenz A
1986–1993	Arbeitsgemeinschaft mit Helmut Dietrich und Much Untertrifaller sen., Bregenz A
1994	Gründung Dietrich|Untertrifaller Architekten, Bregenz A; 2004 Büro Wien A; 2005 Büro St. Gallen CH

Gastprofessuren und Lehraufträge an verschiedenen Universitäten (Konstanz D, Wien A)
Mitglied verschiedener Fachgremien (Architekturstiftung Österreich, Gestaltungsbeirat in Salzburg A und Graz A)

1959	Born in Bregenz, Vorarlberg, A
1979–1988	Studied Architecture at the Vienna University of Technology – graduated under Ernst Hiesmayr
1982–1985	Employed by architectural office of Much Untertrifaller Sr., Bregenz A
1986–1993	Partnership with Helmut Dietrich and Much Untertrifaller Sr., Bregenz A
1994	Founded Dietrich|Untertrifaller Architekten, Bregenz A; 2004 Vienna A office; 2005 St. Gallen CH office

Guest Professor at various universities (Konstanz D, Vienna A)
Member of various expert committees (Austrian Architectural Foundation; Architecture Advisory Committee in Salzburg A and Graz A)

Weitere Informationen/
Further information

dietrich.untertrifaller.com

Partner (seit/since 2008):		Michael Porath, Christof Stäheli, Much Untertrifaller, Helmut Dietrich, Susanne Gaudl, Thomas Spiegel, Peter Nussbaumer (v. l. n. r.)
Bibliografie/ Bibliography	2001	Helmut Dietrich, Much Untertrifaller, Architektur Städtebau Design. Walter Zschokke (Hrsg.). Springer Verlag.
	2008	Rural Urbanism. Feireiss Commerell (Hrsg.). Aedes Berlin. Dietrich|Untertrifaller Architekten. Bauten und Projekte seit 2000. Walter Zschokke (Hrsg.). Springer Verlag.
	2009	ETH Sport Center Science City. Departement Architektur (Hrsg.). gta Verlag.
Werkausstellung/ Exhibitions	seit 2008	*Rural Urbanism*, Meran I, Berlin D, Paris F, Wien A, Zürich CH, Prag CZ, Klagenfurt A, Köln D, Hamburg D
Auszeichnungen/Awards: (Auswahl/Selection)		*Piranesi Preis* (1993), *Staatspreis für Tourismus und Architektur* (1994, 1998 und 2002), *IOC/IAKS-Award* (1999, 2003, 2011), *Bauherrenpreis Österreich* (2000, 2003, 2006 und 2009), *Staatspreis für Architektur und Nachhaltigkeit (2002), Goldenes Verdienstzeichen* Land Wien (2010)

Dietrich|Untertrifaller danken ihren Projektpartnern:

Dietrich|Untertrifaller would like to thank their project partners:

Planungsteam E-Plus	Haustechnikplanung	e-plus.at
gbd	Tragwerksplanung	gbd.at
Hecht	Licht- und Elektroplanung	hecht.at
Omicron	Prüflösungen Energietechnik	omicron.at
Rhomberg	Hoch- und Tiefbau	rhombergbau.at
Roma	Sonnenschutzsysteme	roma.de
Land Vorarlberg	Wirtschaft und Kultur	vorarlberg.at
Weithas	Bauphysik	weithas.com
Ellensohn	Architektur und Bauleitung	ellensohn-architekten.de
team gmi Gasser	Energieeffizienz und Komfort	teamgmi.com
Glas Marte	Glasbau	glasmarte.at
Prisma	Standort- und Regionalentwicklung	prisma-zentrum.com
Rietmann & Partner	Steuerberatung	rietmann-partner.ch
Zech	Türen, Fenster, Klimatechnik	zechfenster.com

Quart Verlag Luzern/Quart Publishers Lucerne

De aedibus international
8 Dietrich | Untertrifaller (dt/e)
7 Geurst & Schulze Architecten (dt/e)
6 Wingender Hovenier Architecten (dt/e)
5 Tony Fretton Architects (dt/e)
4 Jonathan Woolf Architects (dt/e)
3 Hufnagel Pütz Rafaelian (dt/e)
2 Hild und K (dt/e)
1 Stanton Williams (dt/e)

Monografien/Monographs
Sergison Bates architects (dt und e)
Miroslav Šik. Architektur 1988–2012 (dt/e)
Valerio Olgiati (dt und e)
Burkard Meyer. Konkret/Concrete (dt/e)
Gion A. Caminada. Cul zuffel e l'aura dado (dt/e)

Quart Verlag GmbH, Heinz Wirz; Verlag für Architektur und Kunst
Denkmalstrasse 2, CH-6006 Luzern; books@quart.ch, www.quart.ch